Ben Moore

P9-AQC-076

RELIGION YESTERDAY AND TODAY

Religion
Yesterday and Today

By
HENRY SLOANE COFFIN

*Brown Professor of Homiletics and Pastoral
Theology and President of the Faculty, Union
Theological Seminary in the City of New York*

COKESBURY PRESS

NASHVILLE

DISCARD

UNITY SCHOOL LIBRARY
UNITY VILLAGE, MISSOURI 64065

RELIGION YESTERDAY AND TODAY
COPYRIGHT, MCMXL
BY WHITMORE & SMITH

All rights in this book are reserved. No part of the text may be reproduced in any form without written permission of the publishers, except brief quotations used in connection with reviews in a magazine or newspaper.

LC # 40-27567

SET UP, ELECTROTYPED, PRINTED AND BOUND
BY THE PARTHENON PRESS AT NASHVILLE,
TENNESSEE, UNITED STATES OF AMERICA

To

ALEXANDER MARTIN, D.D., LL.D.

Sometime Professor and Principal in New College,
Edinburgh, in whose classroom I began the study
of theology forty-three years ago, and who ever
since has given me his enlightening friendship

PREFACE

THESE six lectures were delivered on the Charles F. Deems Foundation in New York University in the autumn of 1939 and on the Jarrell Foundation in Emory University, Atlanta, Georgia, in January, 1940. Their title, shortened for convenience' sake, should read "Religion Yesterday and Today in a Section of American Protestant Christianity." They attempt to portray some of the factors which influenced thinking among these Christians a half century ago and some of the factors since which have led some of us, their successors, to modify or revise their views. The lectures set forth trends, but they do not venture to predict whither these will lead Tomorrow.

I have of purpose confined myself to that segment of the American Church with which I have been familiar. If I criticize the views of men from whom I learned much, and many of whom enriched me with their friendship, it is because as sturdy liberals they taught me to follow truth first, to expect changes in human thought, and to believe that the honest expression of one's present views was one's contribution to the ultimate victory of truth, which

7

is vaster far than any man's grasp of it. A half century hence, and probably much sooner, the mood and outlook of Today will seem antiquated. Today is not so good that we wish its mood and outlook prolonged. The kaleidoscopic shifting of opinions serves to bring out the abiding worth of Him who holds our loyalty and whose mind for their time every generation of Christians sincerely tries to know and express.

HENRY SLOANE COFFIN

Union Theological Seminary
New York City

CONTENTS

gious instinct?—Effects of the scientific exploration of the religious life—The theology of religious experience and "Humanism"—The reaction against anti-intellectualism—Emphasis upon the Church as the mediator of religious faith—Stress on the "given"—The evidence of Christian experience valid within its sphere

V. THE SOCIAL CONSCIENCE

Prosperity and political corruption—The Christian protest—Settlements and institutional churches—Economic feudalism—The Christian scrutiny of the capitalist system—The social conscience and new emphases in theology—The Great War and Christian ethics—The revolt against liberalism—The fresh attention to the spiritual bases of democracy—The Kingdom of God beyond and in history

VI. THE CHURCH

Concern for children and young people—Effects on church architecture and worship—The Sabbath—Changes in the meaning of the Fatherhood of God and the Lordship of Christ—The revolt against authority—Present changes in emphasis to combat current ideologies—Interest in the Church and Church reunion—The Church in conflict with current social trends—The Church on the defensive and the summons to aggressiveness

Chapter I

EVOLUTIONARY SCIENCE

THE middle-aged and elderly today are homesick. They find themselves in an alien time and keep turning back wistful eyes to the world of their childhood and youth. Every year produces a crop of memoirs which try "to pin down on paper a dear and accustomed way of life" [1] that is gone. Mr. Canby calls it "The Age of Security"—which accounts for the nostalgia of so many, resentful that they no longer feel safe.

An occasional contemporary interpreter of our Yesterday—the 1890's and early 1900's—was aware of the relative absence of danger. C. F. G. Masterman, in a collection of essays entitled *In Peril of Change*, said of his day:

For the first time in many centuries . . . we see a race developing who have experienced nothing but a serene and ordered existence. From the beginning they have been sheltered from the disturbing elements of life. They do not possess imagination necessary to realise that this is an abnormal and transitory phase of the world's development. All their accepted ideas in art, ethics, religion, are inherited from times when this

[1] See page 175 for beginning of references.

11

tranquillity was lacking. They are becoming vaguely conscious that for them the language is strained, extravagant, unreal. They have no conception of such a cosmic upheaval, the disarrangement of a universe, as, for example, the great disturbance of '89 in France or the deliquescence of the whole social order before the invader of 1870. Even Nature's catastrophes have been sedulously removed. There is no fear of great epidemics, and only the occasional remote and unrealised echo of an unexpected destruction as that of Martinique.[2]

Men were at home in an orderly world with no panic fear lurking in the shadows.

But while outward circumstances were so comfortable for the majority in this section of mankind, the thoughtfully devout were by no means at ease. It seemed to them that their spiritual world was tumbling about them. Henry van Dyke lectured to students of divinity at Yale in 1896 on *The Gospel for an Age of Doubt*. And Doubting Castle then was manned by formidable knights: Huxley, Tyndall, W. K. Clifford, Herbert Spencer, and Frederick Harrison among scientific philosophers, Renan and Froude and Morley among historical and literary critics, Zola, Maupassant, and Thomas Hardy with his "Tess" among naturalistic novelists. The Bible, which had held so pre-eminent a place in the faith of Protestant Christians, seemed torn in tatters by the scholars ostensibly expounding its religion. Prof. C. C. Everett of Harvard declared that the last third of the Nineteenth Century witnessed a greater revolution that took place under Luther.[3]

The sense of external security, the preoccupation of men with their increasing mastery of things and its consequent additions to comfort, their absorption in material success, rendered it an unfavorable epoch for advances in the life with God. Henry Adams surveyed all about him a "vast plain of self-content."[4] Among many intellectuals religion was an optional luxury unneeded either for the understanding of the world or for the conduct of life. Among the hosts of the underprivileged, Father Dolling in East London summed up the situation at both sides of the Atlantic when he wrote:

Religion has, so to speak, gone to pieces; there is no opposition; we do not care enough to oppose. God is not in any of our thoughts; we do not even fear Him. We face death with perfect composure, for we have nothing to give up and nothing to look forward to. Heaven has no attraction because we should be out of place there. And Hell has no terrors.[5]

But the vast number of Protestant Christians were troubled believers or half-believers. The religious controversies of the period would not have aroused such public attention had there not been so many who cared. When Mrs. Humphry Ward published her *Robert Elsmere*—a novel whose appeal was solely in its treatment of the difficulties of a young clergyman affected by the current attacks on miracles—between thirty and forty thousand copies were sold in England within nine months, and it continued selling at the rate of seven hundred copies a week; and more than two hundred thousand copies (mostly pirated, for International Copyright did not come for a few years) were sold within a twelvemonth in this country. Mr. Gladstone thought it of such danger to Christianity that he wrote an answer; and the interest here is vividly attested by the following advertisement which appeared about 1890:

TO THE PUBLIC

We beg to announce that we have purchased an edition of the Hyde Park Company's *Robert Elsmere,* and also their edition of *Robert Elsmere and the Battle of Belief*—a criticism by the Right Hon. W. E. Gladstone, M.P.

These two books will be presented to each purchaser of a single cake of Balsam Fir Soap.

Respectfully,

THE MAINE BALSAM FIR CO.[6]

To the folk of our Yesterday, the childhood and youth of many among ourselves, the historic convictions of the Christian religion appeared under furious assault. Timid believers trembled, and even the stalwart wondered would their faith sustain it and come off victorious.

In assessing the factors which were unsettling religious ideas a generation among Protestants a first disturbing force was current scientific views.

Earlier in the Nineteenth Century geology had disputed the age of our planet calculated by Old Testament chronology and printed in many editions of the Bible. In rebuttal defenders of the accuracy of the story of the Creation interpreted the six days in which the Creator toiled as six long aeons. Certain fundamentalists of that time made the ingenious suggestion that fossils, whose discovery upset Biblical computations of time, had been scattered by the devil to shake the faith of believers; but intelligent Christians had been satisfied with the Scripturally approved explanation that one day is with the Lord as a thousand years—or possibly much longer, since finite minds may not grasp fully the Divine arithmetic. But by the 1890's even the rank and file in the churches were confronting Evolution and its conflict with the Biblical account of the way in which God had made all living things. The continuous process of development was presented as automatic and seemingly left no room for the creative and controlling activity of the living God. Interventions, such as miracles and immediate answers to prayer, were excluded. Men, who had thought their race made by the Creator in His own likeness and uniquely related to Him, felt debased when told that human beings had emerged fortuitously from a species akin to the higher apes: "Such hues of hap and hazard Man's Emergence wore." While the more dramatic scenes in the struggle between the exponents of Evolution and the representatives of Christian theology occurred in the Day before our Yesterday, the full force of the new difficulties, then felt only by intellectuals, was now pressing on the minds of hundreds of thousands of would-be Christian men and women.

The autobiographical reminiscences of one of the most read authors of the '90's, John Fiske, portrays what was taking place in the minds of many of those who avidly sought help in his books. He says of the traditional doctrines of God and His world, in which he had been reared:

I can never forget the feeling of revulsion I experienced when I first brought these dogmas together in my mind as an interrelated whole . . . I tried to get clearly before me the scheme of cosmic creation and sustentation which these dogmas set forth; and what a mighty drama of Infinite and finite coexistences stood revealed! Both orders of existences appeared as inextricably inmeshed in a mass of metaphysical assumptions, wherein science was disowned, where reason was discredited, and where blind unquestioning faith was regarded as the only passport to Christian knowledge. Fortunately science was then giving a nobler and a more verifiable knowledge in regard to cosmic creation and the meaning of human life, as well as yielding a far higher conception of the Infinite Power back of the cosmos than could be derived from these dogmas, and I was not long in freeing my mind from their benumbing influence.[7]

Not everyone contrived to adjust his Christian faith and his scientific views. Many found the God of religion incompatible with unmoral Force disclosed in the cosmic process. A Deity who had personal relations with men was incredible. A still larger number, captivated by these scientific explanations of the world and of man, found God fading completely from their horizon. It was not so much that he was unbelievable as irrelevant. The experience of a distinguished and influential Yale professor was representative of thousands in his generation.

William Graham Sumner had been a youth of intense religious interest and was an active Episcopal clergyman when his *alma mater* invited him to a post on her faculty. He taught economics, and later sociology ("societology," he preferred to call it) ; and his mind became absorbed in the study of the development of human institutions—the "folkways," as he labeled them. He had maintained his connections with the Church for a number of years after assuming his professorship, but in the '90's he discontinued them, and later explained what had befallen him by saying:

> I never consciously gave up a religious belief. It was as if I had put my beliefs into a drawer, and when I opened it there was nothing there at all.[8]

Among the thoughtful Agnosticism had numerous adherents. There might be a God, but they could see no connection that He had with existence as they viewed it. He could not be demonstrated by the scientific methods of verification which they trusted to validate other conceptions by which they dealt with reality. Encouraged by the spectacular results of their approach to truth, the representatives of science were apt to assert that it was the sole approach. To observe, to classify the facts, to discover general principles or laws disclosed in them—this became in the Western world the one route to certain knowledge. It was much more effectively taught in schools and colleges than was religion; it spread to non-Christian lands with the educational system and did far more to end faith in their ancestral gods than the missionary propaganda; it secularized education and conditioned minds all over the world.

In this country during the earlier and more bitter clash of Evolution with Religion, Henry Ward Beecher, the most widely known preacher, and President James McCosh of Princeton College, a divine of unquestioned orthodoxy, had been conspicuous leaders who announced that the new scientific doctrine was not hostile to Christian faith. By the beginning of the '90's there were many who shared this outlook, and some who gloried in evolutionary science as an ally of theology. The two Christian interpreters of current science who had the largest following were Henry Drummond and John Fiske.

The former had the ear of Church people by reason of his friendship with Dwight L. Moody, the universally respected evangelist. Drummond entered the lists with a book entitled *Natural Law in the Spiritual World*. It had an enormous vogue, and was translated into every European language except those of Turkey and Greece.[9] It made the realm of religion real to many. The laws of the natural sciences seemed to them demonstrated explanations of the ways of actual existence. If the same laws prevailed in the sphere of the spirit, it, too, was not an illusion. To be sure, the fundamental basis of the book was wrong, as the more acute leaders of the Church at once saw. It reduced the spiritual realm where there is freedom to the level of the physical which is determined. It degraded personality in both God and man. Drummond reversed himself in his Lowell Lectures for 1893 on *The Ascent of Man.* Instead of carrying physical processes into the moral and spiritual worlds, he showed ethical processes at work in regions usually thought to be ruled by merely physical laws. "The struggle for the life of others" is disclosed side by side with "the struggle for life." The Christian law of love appeared to him inwoven in the whole fabric of existence. In Nature he saw clear traces of the Lamb slain from the foundation of the world.

Drummond was not an accurate interpreter of Darwin, who had meant by "the struggle for life" the struggle for the life of the species including its offspring. He read into cells his own feelings and motives, and was a poetic translator of current science. But there is no question of the reassurance which hundreds of believing readers derived from his books, and his religion was a contagious evangelical Christianity.

John Fiske was a more penetrating thinker. He made much of the fact that man seems always to have been religious. He pointed out that all man's other basic traits have developed as responses to his environment, and witness to factors in it to which they correspond. If there be no objective God to whom man's religious nature is a response, this is "something utterly without precedent in the whole history of creation." [10] He viewed the evolutionary process as a vast purposive pageant leading up to the emergence of man. This, he declared, witnessed impressively to the correctness of the Christian conviction of a righteous and faithful Creator:

When from the dawn of life we see all things working together toward the evolution of the highest spiritual attributes of Man, we know, however, the words may stumble in which we try to say it, that God is in the deepest sense a moral Being. The everlasting source of phenomena is none other than the infinite Power that makes for righteousness.[11]

One of his books is captioned *Through Nature to God.*

When almost all the intellectual leaders of the time asserted that the scientific method was the one assured avenue to truth, ministers felt that they must present the Gospel in scientific terms. The public tacitly assumed that all beliefs could be divided into two classes—those which could be verified by

scientific proof, and were therefore convincing; and
those which lacked this proof, and must therefore be
rejected. Book after book came from the press which
attempted to reconcile faith in God with the findings of the scientists. If an eminent biologist or
physicist made a commendatory reference to religion, that was news, and was inserted in the papers
and quoted in hundreds of pulpits. Dr. Lyman Abbott, preacher and editor, declared:

When the whole scientific and intellectual world is
moving in one direction, the minister who is not a
scientist may get himself run over, but he cannot stop
the procession by getting in front of it.[12]

Dr. Newman Smyth, an outstanding theologian,
spent hours in his fifties and sixties in chemical and
biological laboratories "to go to school to nature for
fresh inspiration and larger, serener faith." [13] Dr.
Abbott published an extensively circulated series
of articles on *The Theology of an Evolutionist*.
Like Drummond, he proclaimed:

I believe that the great laws of life which natural
science has elucidated from a study of natural phenomena are analogous to, if not identical with, the laws
of the spiritual life, and that the latter are to be interpreted by the former.[14]

Dr. Smyth, with John Fiske, believed that one could pass "through science to faith." [15]

Sometimes in my own preparation for the pulpit and consequent wrestling with my own questionings of spiritual forces and laws, as well as over the doubts and difficulties of some of my hearers, there has come to me a fresh reassurance and inspiration in turning to my biological studies. Looking into the creative processes of life as made apparent in some of my laboratory slides, I have seemed to grasp some great creative principle or law of life starting from the beginnings of things and reaching on and up to fulfilments passing knowledge.[16]

Unquestionably such scientific study, becoming at that time more common in schools and colleges, banished the older theological dogmatism. Minds were taught to seek truth disinterestedly and to face their findings fearlessly. There was an enfranchisement of the intelligence which stimulated liberalism in all spheres of life. But there was also a new dogmatism. Dr. Abbott declared that

God has but one way of doing things; that His way may be described in one word as the way of growth, or development, or evolution.[17]

That was a narrowing of the message of religion under the tyranny of the popular scientific doctrine of the moment. (It suggests the similar dogmatism

23

on the part of certain theologians today who see God revealing Himself always and only in a dialectic process.) It was to look at the contents of the Bible and the varieties of religious experience with the blinders of a scientific presupposition, as previous generations of divines had viewed them with the presuppositions of a theological creed. For the time being this scientific jargon made religion more cogent, but it impoverished, and to some extent distorted, the Christian Gospel. It identified the God and Father of Jesus Christ with the cosmic process. A poem quoted with tiresome frequency from pulpit after pulpit concludes one verse

Some call it Evolution,
And others call it God.[18]

But many would not call it "God." Its Deity was not the Father and Friend, whose nature is love; and they could neither trust nor adore Him. They were forced to seek a substitute for religion, and some of them felt that science could itself provide that substitute. Intelligent men believed, for example, that an assured basis for a hope of surviving death could be found by establishing contact with spirits in the unseen world. The Society for Psychical Research was formed in Britain and this country, and enrolled a number of university professors and other intellectuals. It patronized various mediums, who claimed to receive and transmit messages from the dead. It published learnedly phrased reports of such seances. But even its most ardent devotees were plagued with the frauds most mediums proved to be, and were obliged to confess a reluctance to "re-entering by a scullery window the heavenly mansion" out of which they had been kicked by the back door.[19] Science appeared to land them in a questionable credulity.

Others, who called Evolution "God," were led by it far from Christian ethics without being aware how remote they were. A phrase like "the survival of the fittest" readily condoned ruthless competition in business and imperialistic aggression in international relations. An America expanding in population and wealth with amazing rapidity felt itself patently among the fittest. An outstanding leader of the churches made this astounding pronouncement, and evidently found it so acceptable to audiences and to readers that he published it word for word in two of his extensively circulated books:

The unoccupied arable lands of the earth are limited and will soon be taken. The time is coming when the pressure of population on the means of subsistence will be felt here, as it is now felt in Europe and Asia. Then will the world enter on a new phase of its history—*the final competition of races, for which the Anglo-Saxon is being schooled.* Long before the thousand millions are here, the mighty centrifugal tendency inherent in this stock and strengthened in the United States will assert itself. Then this race of unequaled energy with all the majesty of numbers and the might of wealth behind it— the representative let us hope of the largest liberty, the purest Christianity, the highest civilization—having developed peculiarly aggressive traits calculated to impress its institutions upon mankind, will spread itself over the earth. And can anyone doubt that the result of this competition of races will be the survival of the fittest?[20]

Such a statement, coming from a recognized Christian leader, and one whose social conscience made him a pioneer in the application of the Gospel to civic and industrial affairs, shows the warping of the principles of Christ wrought by this interpretation of Christianity in the light of current views of science. Such opinions prevalent in the early nineties paved the way for the imperialism which embarked on and followed the War with Spain.

A wholesome warning to the confident users of scientific terms was given by the British statesman, Arthur Balfour, when he pointed out that if religion was disparaged for inexact and symbolic language in its description of God's life with men, scientific words were no less picturesque portrayals of the processes of nature.

The universe as represented to us by science is wholly unimaginable, and our conception of it is what in Theology would be termed purely anthropomorphic.[21]

This was a skillful turning of their own weapons upon the rather shallow assailants of Christian convictions in the name of assured scientific accuracy. It anticipated the position repeatedly taken by more recent scientists that all their language is man's attempt to picture processes in nature as they appear to him. They may differ as much from our common-sense view of things as the wave-lengths of ethereal vibrations physicists measure are unlike the colors our eyes see; but our colors are no more symbolic than are the waves and vibrations of the physicists.

A more trenchant attack on those who were grounding faith in God on the evolutionary process came from thinkers who questioned whether it really yielded the meanings which such men were reading from it. William James, the psychologist and philosopher, spoke of these interpreters as "tender-minded." They were romanticists rather than realists. The "tough-minded," like himself, discerned no advancing movement in the natural world, only "the driftings of the cosmic atoms," "a kind of aimless weather, doing and undoing."

Nature has no one distinguishable ultimate tendency with which it is possible to feel a sympathy.[22]

There was a serious danger in finding God in the processes of nature. The older interpreters had looked on this as a fallen world, and nature as well as man was involved in evil. Evolutionary theologians gaily spoke of the Fall as "a tumble up." Evil was good in the making, and without evil goodness could not be. Dr. George A. Gordon said that for John Fiske sin and holiness were "Siamese twins whose being is inseparable." [23] Both were essential in the drama of human development. If one went "through nature to God," one arrived at a Deity of highly questionable character.

It has never been an easy matter for Christianity to combine the God of redemption known through Christ and the God of nature. The thinkers who went "through science to faith" began with the creation. They made little of sin. Evil was inherent in the production of character; it was good in the making. Another and much profounder Christian school began with the God who had revealed Himself fully in Jesus Christ. They started with the fact that they had been laid hold on by this Figure. In

Him God unveiled Himself to them. Lecturing at Yale in 1903 Dr. George W. Knox, a forceful representative of this position, insisted:

The procedure is not from nature's God to the Christian's. . . . The Christian finds his God in nature because he finds Him first in Christ and in his own heart, and then interprets nature in accordance with Him who is thus known.[24]

Science and religion fill two different functions. It is idle to talk of going through science to Christian faith.

Science has as its task the classification of that which is and has been, religion the embodiment of the highest, of that which is not yet in the natural order, but shall be.[25]

If we go through nature to God, we reach not the Christian Deity, but a submoral, infrapersonal Energy. Nature is still unredeemed. It is groaning and travailing in pain waiting to be subdued to a divine purpose by sons of God. Both in human affairs and in the physical cosmos which is their scene and setting, and with which man is in part akin and in part at variance, a real battle is on. Redeemed men with God are called to subdue all things unto His kingdom.

The ideal [to quote Dr. Knox again] is not found in the brute fact, but is brought to it, and the brute fact is made its servant, and is thereby transformed and glorified.[26]

The revelation in nature is not discarded, although of itself it is ambiguous. But God is found, or rather men are found by Him, first in Christ. Then the universe and all history become luminous with His presence, and add to our thought of God's greatness, wisdom, and power.

This anticipates the position of Today among many of the thoughtfully devout. To be sure, intellectuals in all lands and masses of ordinary folk are still bound by the outlook of a former generation and consider the scientific method the only path to truth.[27] This is the dogma of anti-religious movements the world over and the assumption upon which much of our secular system of education is based. But many foremost scientists insist that their method of grasping reality is a net through whose meshes slip many facts, and those among the most important for man's life. They are often men of Christian faith and witnesses to God who has come to them along another path. And generally science is casting no such spell over our day as it did over its predecessor, for it is plain that its discoveries may ruin as well as bless mankind.

Contemporary Christians wish to be both scientific and religious, but we are not trying to combine science and religion, for to us they are two distinct roads to reality. Scientists may tell us that the result of their investigations leaves them with an impression of the mysterious background of the cosmos not incompatible with the Christian interpretation. They may report the inference of a Mind behind phenomena;[28] but it is at most an inference, nor can they infer whether the world-spirit be good or evil. Science cannot furnish a clue to history nor an ethical standard. Its methods of research are an austere and rigorous school for some virtues unhappily not always learned in the household of faith. A Christian may be both a wiser and a better Christian if he is trained in these methods. But it is in the school of Christ that men receive the motives and consecration without which the powers conferred by science may become factors for annihilating the civilization that scientists with the Christian tradition most wish to preserve and advance.

The opinion of Christian thinkers today, both Protestant and Roman Catholic, is admirably expressed in one of the last letters of Baron von Hugel:

All science . . . is the ceaseless seeking, the ceaseless restating, the ceaseless discovering of error, and the substituting of something nearer the truth. I do not see how science can be asked to start with a definite God. . . . I think it cannot even end with more than a vague reverence and a sense of a deep background. . . . Religion on the contrary begins with a full affirmation of a Reality, other and more than all mankind. . . . Assimilate religion to science and you have leveled down to something which though excellent for science has taken from religion its entire force and good. . . . Force science up to the level of religion, or think that you have done so, and science affirms far more than, as such, it can affirm, and you, on your part, are in a world of unreality.[29]

Today the Christian task is neither to combat science nor to reconcile the findings of theologians with those of the scientists; but to deal with secularism, which now lacks a convincing intellectual basis, and which thousands are finding incapable of affording them a satisfactory explanation of the world or inspiration to live in it. The void in which naturalism left men, without meaning in existence and without anything to claim their loyalty and devotion, has been filled for many by substitute religions—nationalism, racialism, allegiance to class. These deifications of the human cannot stand up under intelligent investigation, but appeal to primitive emotions in people under dire fear or economic pressure, and for the time being give their devotees a sense of cosmic importance as members of a community with a momentous destiny. As these ideologies prove themselves both intellectually and practically inadequate, religion has, and will have increasingly, its chance as the one hope for the human race in a desperate age.

For Yesterday possessed another confident hope. It was customary in the nineties to speak of the weariness of the *fin de siecle;* but this was partly a pose, for there was an almost universal and boundless faith in progress. Indeed faith in progress and the resolve to do something toward furthering it was the religion of many—a genuine substitute for faith in God. Almost everyone thought of himself, and wished others to think of him, as progressive. "Forward-looking" was a complimentary expression for the type of man desired for any important post. The conception of Evolution was unquestionably a chief factor in producing this faith.

Strictly speaking, it had nothing to do with either material or moral progress. Evolution is a term for a process by which certain biological changes occur in response to stimuli and develop new forms of life. One cannot say that a later form is better than an earlier; it is better adapted to the later environment. In the evolution of the horse successive generations may "stand more and more on tiptoe," [30] but *Eohip-*

pus with four toes may be more useful for certain purposes than present-day horses with hooves. Unfortunately moral terms were confused with scientific terms which connote merely change. In a letter to Lyell, Mr. Darwin had allowed himself to speak of "Natural Selection, and as a general consequence, Natural Improvement." [31] So both in the popular mind and among more careful thinkers Evolution became synonymous with progress.

It was this which made men embrace it as a gospel and use it as a clue to the meaning of life and destiny. Herbert Spencer confesses in his *Autobiography:*

Once having become possessed by the conception of evolution in its comprehensive form, the desire to elaborate and set it forth was so strong that to have passed life in doing something else would, I think, have been almost intolerable.[32]

Here is what Evolution meant to him as he contemplated "the great laws of existence":

Growth is unceasing; and though slow, all powerful; showing itself here in some rapidly developing outline, and there where necessity is less, exhibiting only the fibrils of incipient organization. Irresistible as it is subtle, he sees in the workings of these changes a power that bears onwards peoples and governments, regardless of their theories, and schemes, and prejudices—a power which sucks the life out of their landed institutions, shrivels up their state parchments with a breath, paralyzes long venerated authorities, obliterates the most deeply graven laws, makes statesmen recant and puts prophets to the blush, buries cherished customs, shelves precedents, and which, before men are conscious of the fact, has wrought a revolution in all things, and filled the world with a higher life. Always towards perfection is the mighty movement—towards a complete development and more unmixed good; subordinating in its universality all petty irregularities and fallings back, as the curvature of the earth subordinates mountains and valleys. Even in evils the student learns to recognize only a struggling beneficence.[33]

Is it any marvel that the youthful Beatrice Webb, inserting this rhapsody in her diary, exclaims: "Who could wish for a grander faith than this"?[34] Such faith was good news.

The enormous technological advances of their day went to men's heads. There seemed no limit to what might be in store. Alfred Russel Wallace, co-discoverer with Darwin of the principle of natural selection, published a retrospect in 1898 of *The Wonderful Century*, through seven decades of which he had lived. He was not blind to its ethical defects —indeed he was more discerning than most of his contemporaries of the social injustices which deprived millions of any share in the splendid gains which he recorded.   But his retrospect ends almost lyrically:

The flowing tide is with us. We have great poets, great writers, great thinkers, to cheer and guide us; and an ever-increasing band of earnest workers to spread the light and help on the good time coming. And as this century has witnessed a material and intellectual advance wholly unprecedented in the history of human progress, so the coming century will reap the full fruition of that advance in a moral and social upheaval of an equally new and unprecedented kind and equally great in amount.[35]

The moral and social upheaval has come; but how different is the tone and outlook today when more than a third of the century has run its course! None of us believes that the cosmic process is an escalator carrying mankind inevitably upward. We may be headed downward toward an unimaginable catastrophe. Our time is already witnessing brutalities we had not thought possible. An age even more barbarous may be in prospect.

Professor Whitehead, surveying the scientific development of the Nineteenth Century, noted an alteration in the attitude toward change. The first half of the century was "a peculiar period of hope." Sixty or seventy years later he detects "a note of disillusionment, or at least of anxiety." [36]   The *fin de siecle* weariness was partly pose and partly due to the alarming discovery that its hope stood on a dubious foundation.   In 1893 Mr. Huxley delivered a lecture at Oxford, calculated to make believers in progress pause and think.   He pointed out the conflict between nature's ways and the ethical principles by which men try to live in society and said:

Let us understand, once for all, that the ethical progress of society depends, not on imitating the cosmic process, still less in running away from it, but in combating it.[37]

He was sanguine that men could successfully do this for a long, long while.   But it would not be forever.

If for millions of years our globe has taken the upward road, yet, sometime, the summit will be reached and the downward route will be commenced.[38]

His words were hardly listened to, and certainly not seriously believed by an incurably optimistic public which much preferred to fuddle its mind by reading Maeterlinck with his expectations of continuous happinesses flocking toward them:

It seems as though we heard those movements; the sound of superhuman footsteps, an enormous door opening, a breath caressing us, or light coming; we do not know; but expectation at this pitch is an ardent and marvelous state of life, the fairest period of happiness.[39]

The door opened and the most frightful war in history was upon them, and with others in its train. The superhuman footsteps were those of bloody Mars. Today we listen to the Huxley of 1893 when he says in the name of science:

The cosmic nature born with us and, to a large extent, necessary for our maintenance, is the outcome of millions of years of severe training, and it would be folly to imagine that a few centuries will suffice to subdue its masterfulness to purely ethical ends.[40]

Men as individuals and men in groups—for nations, races, classes, even churches, often seem far worse than the individuals who compose them—must be made over. Nor will time, even centuries or aeons of it, do this. It is the task of religion to change and to renew characters—the minds and characters of men and of societies. The propaganda of idolatrous religions is doing it through the school system, the radio, the press, the theater, mass demonstrations, and every means it can ingeniously employ. The results are patent in the infamies perpetrated by Germany and Russia. Christianity must gird itself, as it did in the early days, and has done again in its most vigorous missionary periods in many lands, to create a true Christendom—a world community ruled by the mind of Christ. The shattering of the faith in automatic progress, the realization that there is nothing in nature of itself which can save or help mankind and much that may destroy it, the appalling menace of the tribal gods of deified nation and race and class, is turning the thought of man wistfully to the God who is above and other than the cosmic forces or man-made divinities. Our contemporaries are open to receive the good news of the God of the Christian heritage who is Redeemer and Lord both of men and of the world. No readings of the ongoings of nature give complete views of His workings. Neither fears nor hopes based on them are relevant to faith in One "who is able to do exceeding abundantly above all that we ask or think." The truest religion of Today is bidding believers tell themselves: "My soul, wait thou only upon God, for my expectation is from Him."

Chapter II

THE DIVINE IMMANENCE

THE conception of God which held thoughtful Christians of Yesterday differs from that which is appealing to thoughtful Christians Today. Various factors, one of which was evolutionary science, had made them revolt from and break with the conception of God in which they had been reared. They had been taught to think of Him as the sovereign Lord of the universe, who ruled over and judged them. John Fiske, whose childhood was passed in Middletown, Connecticut, has left a vivid description of the view of God which his religious training in home and church gave him when he was a boy:

I imagined a narrow office just over the zenith, with a tall standing-desk running lengthwise, upon which lay several open ledgers bound in coarse leather. There was no roof over this office, and the walls rose scarcely five feet from the floor, so that a person standing at the desk could look out upon the whole world. There were two persons at the desk—a tall, slender man of aquiline features, wearing spectacles, with a pen in his hand and another behind his ear, was God. The other, whose appearance I do not distinctly recall, was an at-

40

tendant angel. Both were diligently watching the deeds of men and recording them in the ledgers. To my infant mind this picture was not grotesque, but ineffably solemn, and the fact that all my words and acts were thus written down, to confront me at the day of judgment, seemed naturally a matter of grave concern.[1]

This Deity outside of and above the world Fiske as a student at Harvard exchanged for a Deity who was the Soul of the world, the Energy and Life manifest in the cosmic process and supremely in the conscience of man.

At the other side of the Atlantic W. Hale White, a student of divinity, busied day after day with the dry bones of the current traditional Calvinism in a very "sound" seminary, tells us:

I happened to find a volume of poems in paper boards. It was called *Lyrical Ballads,* and I read first one and then the whole book. It conveyed to me no new doctrine. . . . It excited a movement and a growth which went on till, by degrees, all the systems which enveloped me like a body gradually decayed from me and fell away into nothing.[2]

His experience suggests another factor which discontented men with the conception of God then current in Protestant Christianity—the Romantic Movement. Its poets felt nature alive with a Divine

Presence which gave them (in Wordsworth's familiar lines)

> a sense sublime
> Of something far more deeply interfused,
> Whose dwelling is the light of setting suns,
> And the round ocean and the living air,
> And the blue sky, and in the mind of man.

The philosophical thought of the middle years of the Nineteenth Century had a strong drift toward *immanentism*. God was the indwelling Being who animates the universe. Men communed with Him by contemplating nature or looking into their own souls. Two of the quotations which preachers of the nineties wore threadbare were Mrs. Browning's

> Earth's crammed with heaven
> And every common bush afire with God;

and Tennyson's

Speak to Him, thou, for He hears, and Spirit with
  Spirit can meet—
Closer is He than breathing, and nearer than hands
  and feet.

God's nearness came as a fresh discovery to men who had been brought up to reverence the Most High enthroned above the world. Washington

Gladden, in the final pages of his *Recollections,* dwells on this as the most important aspect of God which his life had brought to him:

He is near us, in the very breath of our life, in the thrill of our nerves, in the pulsations of our hearts, in the movements of our minds, living and working in us and manifesting himself in every natural force, in every law of life. This is the truth which the world is beginning to understand, the truth of the immanent God; and when it gets to be a reality we shall not be afraid of losing our religion.[3]

Dr. Lyman Abbott harps upon the same chord that

God is truly in the universe, and manifests Himself through all the multifarious forces of nature; that what we call laws of nature are the laws of God's own being; that the activities of nature are the methods of the divine; that God works out the creation from within, thus revealing Himself by the continual forthputting of His wisdom and His power.[4]

These preachers were representative of a great many ministers who read widely and tried to keep abreast of contemporary philosophy.

The Christian Church, with some of the loftiest passages of the Old Testament before it, had always taught God's omnipresence. He is active in every nook of His universe and in every soul of man. But immanence implies a more intimate relationship than omnipresence—that the universe and man are in some sort one with God, and share in His divinity. Omnipresence magnifies God; immanence exalts nature and man. God, nature, and man are all bound together in the closest unity. Devout folk found satisfaction in that oneness. No lines were oftener heard in pulpits than Tennyson's:

> Flower in the crannied wall,
> I pluck you out of the crannies,
> I hold you here, root and all, in my hand,
> Little flower—but *if* I could understand
> What you are, root and all, and all in all,
> I should know what God and man is.

One would think that nothing could be learned from a flower but life in the vegetable world. One could understand no more of God or man than that in their being which they share with this subpersonal realm. The vegetable aspects of God and man do not impress us as particularly significant. What is distinctive of man, and what is distinctive of God, cannot be understood from a flower. But to the immanentist there is a divineness in a flower. It has a spiritual quality. It has mystic roots. So to understand it "root and all, and all in all," takes one into the indwelling presence of God resident within nature—the life of its life, the *Anima mundi*—the Soul of the world.

When men viewed God and nature in such vital association, what were called "natural laws"—the observed cycles in which planets and atoms, plants and creatures, move and live—were regarded as disclosures of God's creative life. These are the ways in which He works. And "laws" were not just statistical calculations arrived at by careful investigators—calculations similar to those on which actuaries construct their tables and by which they predict probable expectations; they were divine forces. They were spoken of as "governing" or "working." They took the place of the angels in ancient Jewish thought—the celestial agents by whom God made and ruled and carried on His universe. One could trust "natural laws," and work with them, and have a devout attitude toward them. This was "the religion of science," so often acclaimed.

And because these methodical processes were divine, everything that happens in nature is a miracle.

All nature and all life is one great theophany. . . . There are not occasional interventions in the order of life which bear witness to the presence of God, but life is itself a perpetual witness to His presence.[5]

God is no occasional visitor; He resides in His world. Some were trying to show that God interposed at special steps in the evolutionary process—in the entrance of life into the inanimate world, in the endowment of man with reason and conscience, in the regeneration of man by the Spirit of God. But this drew a protest from evolutionary theologians:

> If God is only to be left to the gaps in our knowledge, where shall we be when these gaps are filled up? And if they are never to be filled up, is God only to be found in the disorders of the world? Those who yield to the temptation to reserve a point here and there for special divine interposition are apt to forget that this virtually excludes God from the rest of the process. If God appears periodically, He disappears periodically. If He comes upon the scene at special crises, He is absent from the scene in intervals. Whether is all-God or occasional-God the nobler theory? [6]

And because all life is miraculous in this sense of being indwelt by and manifesting God, events like the miraculous incidents of the Bible have no distinctive significance for religion. They were disbelieved as contrary to the laws of nature; they had originated in the minds of pre-scientific people and been recorded by writers without our canons of history. Even had they occurred, they disclosed no special revelation of God, since He is as much in the ordinary events in nature and human history, as in the spectacular and unusual. Dr. Martineau

thought Him more in the ordinary happenings than
in the unique:

> The customs of Heaven ought surely to be more sa-
> cred in our eyes than its anomalies; the dear old ways,
> of which the Most High is never tired, than the strange
> things which He does not love well enough ever to
> repeat.[7]

On that basis the average man is more divine than
the singular Man of Nazareth, and the birth of all
babies more sacred than the Incarnation which took
place only once.

Dr. Martineau had overstated his position; but
he and many of his contemporaries believed every
man divine. Man was the climax of the evolutionary process and the supreme disclosure of the indwelling Creative Spirit of the cosmos. He was still
hampered by his animal inheritance which he had
not yet completely thrown off. But that will more
and more disappear.

> Man is slowly passing from a primitive social state
> in which he is little better than a brute, toward an ulti-
> mate social state in which his character shall have be-
> come so transformed that nothing of the brute can be
> detected in it.[8]

Man is a creature of unlimited possibilities; he is

the spirit
God meant should mate His with an infinite range.[9]

Many who abandoned religion maintained a romantic confidence in man. A British colonial administrator tells us that he gave up Theistic faith as childish, but he sets down his conviction

that there is just a hope, a faint struggling hope [he admits] that Mankind, united in purpose, striving to create and maintain better and better control over this Planet, over the fate and welfare of its own species, may stave off eventual annihilation, may even make itself (millions or billions of years ahead) master of the Solar system.

And he adds (needlessly, one might think) : "Farther than that I need not project my thoughts." [10] Thomas Hardy urged his contemporaries to face

life with dependence placed
On the human heart's resource alone,
In brotherhood bonded close and graced
With lovingkindness fully blown,
And visioned help unsought, unknown.[11]

In Christian circles where the immanentist view was accepted there was a similar confidence in man. John Fiske declared:

According to Mr. Spencer, the divine energy which is manifested throughout the knowable universe is the same energy which wells up in us as consciousness. Speaking for myself, I can see no insuperable difficulty in the notion that at some period in the evolution of Humanity this divine spark may have acquired sufficient concentration and steadiness to survive the wreck of material forms and endure forever. Such a crowning wonder seems to me no more than the fit climax to a creative work that has been ineffably beautiful and marvelous in all its myriad stages.[12]

Dr. Rainsford tells of a meeting of a club of Episcopal clergymen, where he read a paper on "Faith," and a discussion followed. After a number had spoken appreciatively, Dr. W. R. Huntington solemnly rose and said:

In the paper and the discussion of it, one all-important thing—the ultimate basis of authority—has been forgotten. The ultimate basis of authority is the Throne of Almighty God.

To which Dr. Percy Stickney Grant at once replied:

Yes, Dr. Huntington, but where is the Throne of Almighty God if not here [touching his breast] in the heart of man? [13]

That generation thought that Christian men had been groveling before a Despot, and with their immanentist theology they proclaimed in a favorite

49

text of Phillips Brooks: "Son of man, stand upon thy feet." Extremists among them asserted with R. J. Campbell, in the days when he set English Nonconformity by the ears with his *New Theology:*

Jesus was God, but so are we. He was God because His life was the expression of divine love; we too are one with God in so far as our lives express the same thing.[14]

Many preachers spoke of the "humanness" or "humanity" of God. This seemed to them the description which rendered Him most appealing. They and their hearers regarded it as a complimentary characterization of Deity.

Where such opinions were held, there was a break with the older conceptions of what religion had to do for man. He needed no grace to change him and make him "a new creature"; he needed an awakening to what he really is. In his *Religion of a Mature Mind* (a significant title) Dr. George A. Coe wrote:

There can be no higher destiny or duty for men than just to be our whole selves. Expressed in terms of theology, this is nothing more than the experience of the immanent God. It is at once faith and sight. For the practical effect of faith is that we find ourselves at home where we are by assuming that God is there with us. And what more can seeing do? What we need, and what we are coming to find, is the God within the commonplace.[15]

This laid no emphasis on regeneration either of the individual or of society. (It is fair to Dr. Coe to recall that in his later books he has advocated very radical social change.)

This immanentist faith in the divineness of man and of the commonplace—the regular ongoings of human life and thought—fitted in with a current glorification of man's achievements. Modern civilization was naively regarded as a signal blessing. It was often mentioned in the same breath with Christianity. Missionaries were said to spread *the Gospel and civilization.* An Oxford professor of philosophy declared in the words of the Russian, Turgenieff: "I believe in civilization, and I require no further creed." [16] In Christian circles it was felt to be an imperative obligation to adapt the Church—its theology, its ethics, its methods—to the times. A group of Roman Catholics, issuing *The Programme of Modernism,* defined their position as

an attitude which we consider to be simply that of Christians and Catholics who live in harmony with the spirit of their day.[17]

A distinguished Protestant scholar concluded a se-

ries of lectures on modern religious ideas with the
statement:

> We may fairly hope that . . . there will be a growing
> adaptation between Christianity and the world in which
> it lives. The Church has commonly been slow to
> change—a great institution necessarily is. But in the
> end it has always adjusted itself to the ethical and intel-
> lectual tendencies of the age. Had it not, it would
> long ago have perished from the earth. That Chris-
> tianity continues to reveal this adaptability to the de-
> veloping mind of man is a proof that it is alive and
> not dead, and is the best guarantee of its permanent
> influence and power.[18]

William James, despite his assertion elsewhere that
he was "a crass supernaturalist," [19] in his reply to a
questionnaire on his personal religion, said that he
thought of God as "a more powerful Ally of my own
ideals." [20]

It did not occur to these earnest Christians that
there might be something faulty in the spirit of their
day and in their own ideals, that the ethical and intellectual tendencies of the age might not be a divine
standard to which the Christian Church should be
adjusted, that the mind of man might be developing
in ungodly directions. An earlier generation had
looked on themselves as members of a fallen race
with minds and consciences corrupted by sin. This

generation thought of themselves as moving upward, away from a brutal past, where tiger and ape had dominated human nature, toward a future when men should be as God. So profound and keen a thinker as Professor Harnack identified the God of Jesus with his own loftiest aspirations. He concludes his study of *The Essence of Christianity* with this personal confession:

If with a steady will we affirm the forces and the standards which on the summits of our inner life shine out as our highest good, nay, as our real self; if we are earnest and courageous enough to accept them as the great Reality and direct our lives by them; and it we then look at the course of mankind's history, follow its upward development, and search, in strenuous and patient service, for the communion of minds in it, we shall not faint in weariness and despair, but become certain of God, of the God whom Jesus called His Father, and who is also our Father.[21]

A future President of the United States imbibed this immanentist philosophy in the classroom of the eloquent Prof. Charles E. Garman of Amherst College, in the nineties. Of the period when he was climbing the ladder of state politics in Massachusetts, Calvin Coolidge said:

I have always remembered how Garman told his

classes that if they would go along with events, and have the courage and industry to hold to the main stream without being washed ashore by the immaterial cross currents, they would some day be men of power.[22]

There were issues to this immanentist thought which these Christians did not suspect. One arose from this identification of God with man at his loftiest. If man at his highest is divine, what need is there for another Deity? President George Harris of Amherst, speaking of *A Century's Change* in religious thought, noted,

a more cheerful hope that evil may be reduced and eventually removed by human endeavor.[23]

But if man can redeem himself and his world, God seems superfluous. Shortly there appeared a movement, with adherents even in church circles, which borrowed the name of an earlier group of thinkers of the Renaissance, and called itself "Humanism." Like the Positivists, it made Man its divinity. "God" became with the more traditionally Christian among them the spirit of humanity symbolically personified, as "Uncle Sam" or "John Bull" are personifications of the spirits of their peoples, or "Santa Claus" of the spirit of Christmas. Humanism insisted on the scientific approach to reality as the sole pathway to truth and had unquestioning confidence in man's capacity to develop control of his cosmic environment. A well-known professor of theology, still holding the hypothesis of the Christian God, was frank to admit that this hypothesis might be only temporary:

We are quite willing to recognize that our conceptions of physical reality are symbolic rather than descriptive. Nevertheless so long as we can use them in our actual dealings with the world, we have no practical doubts as to the objective existence of the world. If any particular conception comes to be involved in too great difficulties, we simply modify it, or even abandon it for another. Is not the case somewhat similar in the realm of religion? If the theistic hypothesis becomes too difficult to maintain, may we not abandon it for some more suitable conception without abandoning our belief in *some* kind of cosmic reality capable of stimulating in us the experience which we call religion? [24]

The Lord was not to him a "dwelling place in all generations," but a boardinghouse which would serve him until it became inconvenient, when he expected to move to more suitable quarters.

Another Christian theologian made this definition of Deity:

God is precisely that object, whatsoever its nature

may be, which will yield maximum security and abundance to all human living, when right adjustment is made. With this definition of the term it cannot be doubted that God exists. The exact nature of God is still problematical and may be for many years to come.[25]

But the essence of historic Christianity is that God has made known His nature. An inert Something to which man must make adjustment and discover Its nature is not the living Father who in Christ comes to seek His children. Immanentism in these forms had broken with the Christian tradition.

Another unanticipated outcome of immanentism took place overseas. The divine immanence can be as readily—some would say far more readily—combined with paganism. If God be identified with the Life-Force, the vital necessities of a nation or race may become its final tests of truth and right. In an organic theory of society, in which its individual members have meaning only in relation to the whole, the biological element of blood and race may be viewed as the bearer of the folk's destiny in the cosmos. Much of the philosophy now popular in Nazi Germany may be traced back to the immanentism held both here and there a generation ago.

Still another unexpected outcome of immanentism was a revolt against Christian ethics. Among Anglo-

THE DIVINE IMMANENCE

Saxons in the latter years of the Nineteenth Century, even where Christian belief was given up, Christian standards of conduct were usually cherished. Men who thought the heavens empty believed in "the Christ ideal." Frederic Myers recalls George Eliot talking to him "with terrible earnestness" of God, Immortality, Duty, and explaining "how inconceivable the first, how unbelievable the second, and yet how peremptory and absolute the third." [26] And Duty for George Eliot was always conceived in Christian terms. But Christian morality in any time embraces specific obligations and prohibitions only remotely related to the Figure on the pages of the Gospels. Men who considered their own loftier impulses divine found much in the traditional Christian code cramping. A word was borrowed from the study of primitive religions, then popular, and many contemporary Christian commandments were labeled "taboos." Self-realization was deemed the true law of life, and taboos must not be suffered to interfere with this. A philosophy of education was built upon the principle that every life should fully express itself. The War, in which millions of young men were taught to violate the Christian principles in which they had been reared, did much to break down Christian morality and set them to follow this other standard of self-fulfilment.[27] Many of its devotees were unaware that they were parting with Christianity. Their minds were confused because they had little accurate knowledge of the historic Christian faith and life, and had been led to find the divine in their own best selves.

A similar confusion ensued in social ethics. Professor John Bascom, a popular sociologist, taught:

The true synthesis of the universe of God, physical and spiritual, is the kingdom of heaven.[28]

But as Huxley had already pointed out this synthesis was impossible on the basis of current readings of the physical world. A pioneer in the social interpretation of Christianity, Canon Fremantle, said that the kingdom of God was to have its realization "in a progressively righteous state in this world." [29] That view was almost universal among preachers of a Christian social order. Men's ideals of justice and brotherhood were forthwith identified with the reign of God. It was not suspected that man's best dreams would come far short of satisfying the righteousness of God, and that any social order of man's design would stand under His judgment. The complacent optimism of the period led ministers at the dawn of the new century to make such unbelievably shallow utterances, so cheapening to Jesus' own demands, as that of Dr. Hillis in Plymouth pulpit:

> Laws are becoming more just, rulers humane; music is becoming sweeter and books wiser; homes are happier, and the individual heart becoming at once more just and gentle. . . . For today art, industry, invention, literature, learning, and government—all these are captives marching in Christ's triumphant procession up the hill of fame.[30]

And in little more than a decade they were marching to the most destructive war thus far in the bloody annals of human history. With startled and horrified eyes a smug generation saw the hideous and terrifying forces behind its lauded civilization. Its world seemed more Satanic than divine. Immanentism was discarded, for where was a worshipful God in the trends and tendencies which produced this holocaust? Christian thinkers welcomed a book from a German theologian, Rudolf Otto, first published in the dark days of 1917, which represented God as the *ganz anderes,* far above man, whose presence filled him with devout trembling and a sense of creatureliness.[31] God ceased to be "man's giant shadow hailed divine"; He became the transcendent, incomprehensible, awe-ful Lord, both fascinating in His love, and terrible in love's wrath with the unloving. This was reinforced by the writings of von Hugel, which were influential with theologians both in Britain and this country, and who found religion

in a sense of sin, a sense of an immense over-against-ness, of a huge Other before which (man) felt . . . a nothing.[32]

Devout men despaired of finding within the process of civilization, which had issued in this frightful catastrophe, the God who could save them and their world and be the Object of their loyalty and their reliance.

This revolt against immanentism occurred in Europe and Britain more swiftly than here, where the full horrors of the War were imperfectly realized and where for another decade the country enjoyed prosperity. The Humanist movement came to flower here in the 1920's; and it required the Depression and consequent feeling of impotence to bring home to most Americans the sense that man has not unlimited latent powers and must accept his finitude and acknowledge the sinfulness of his best thought and effort before the holy God. He must not think of himself as the proud builder of the kingdom of heaven. If it was of his building, it would not be the kingdom of God. He must learn to distrust his own ideals as vitiated by self-interest and conceit.

He must constantly review them before the searching judgment of God revealed in Christ. A sense of human insufficiency is now for us indispensable to any experience we call Christian. Our hope is placed not in powers within ourselves, but in forces of truth and love outside and above us in which we can participate. We rely upon the Spirit of God who comes upon us, when we submit ourselves to Christ, purifying our motives, renewing our minds, and supplying fresh outreach and energy with which to share in a purpose which is not our own but God's.

It is, however, devoutly to be desired that the preaching of the transcendence of God will not be pushed with us to the lengths which certain of its European prophets, notably Karl Barth and his disciples, are pushing it. The last two generations with their emphasis upon the divine immanence have made an enrichment, if overstated, of the Christian thought of God. They have uncovered for us truth with which we cannot part.

(1) The doctrine of the divine immanence is an insight into His presence as the cohesive factor in nature and man. God is the integrating life of the cosmos—that which renders it a *universe*. The existence of every man and of everything depends upon Him, in whom all live and move and have their be-

ing. Science assumes that the cosmos is intelligible to the human mind. This implies a common spiritual basis. The world is an organic whole, not a mechanism whose parts have been put together. But the world is not a closed system: it is open Godward, and from Him we look for fresh creative activities. It is not merely in the unfolding of latent powers, although these doubtless exist, that we expect future developments, but in fresh advents of the living God, who is *over,* as well as *in,* all.

(2) The doctrine of divine immanence rightly asserts a divine element in man. The youthful Elihu in the *Book of Job* is not a profound thinker, but he voices the faith of the whole company of devout folk who inherit the Biblical tradition when he says:

There is a spirit in man
And the breath of the Almighty giveth him understanding.

Were there not in man at his worst the capacity to perceive and respond to truth, God Himself could not speak to him. Emerson was right when he spoke of man as "a candidate for truth." [33] If our immediate predecessors thought too highly of human capacities, minimizing both man's finiteness and his sin, it is also an exaggeration to say with Middleton Murry:

This is the real beginning of the Christian spiritual life today—the bitter knowledge that we are an evil nothingness.[34]

There is something in every man with which God can start, although apart from Him we may be nothing. The Lord of heaven and earth is undoubtedly unlike us, therefore we must neither flatter ourselves nor debase Him by speaking of His humanity; but He is not *totally* unlike us. Along with the vast difference, which many of our predecessors overlooked, there is a kinship between the Most High and limited and sinful man, or He could not enter into fellowship with us.

(3) The doctrine of divine immanence, which broke down the false division between the sacred and the secular, and made men appreciate the arts and sciences, the gains of technology and commerce, as gifts of God, is a true interpretation of the breadth of the work of His Spirit in mankind. That all these may be tragically misemployed in no way makes them less, in themselves, God's endowments of our race. It would be a sorry day were science and invention, art and business, to be viewed as unrelated to religion. Asceticism has its place, and unquestionably self-discipline for service, involving the ab-

negation of many of life's goods, is essential in some of the highest callings; but the New Testament writer who declared, "God giveth richly all things to enjoy," seems a correct interpreter of the Figure portrayed in the Gospels. It is the purpose and spirit with which art or investigation or any industry is enterprised, which renders it divine or diabolic. The capacities of reason and appreciation and skill, all man's native and acquired powers which produce a culture, are in themselves gifts of God.

But self-sufficiency has been the ruin of civilization after civilization. In pride the prophets have seen the seed of destruction. "Thou saidst in thine heart . . . I will exalt my throne above the stars of God. . . . I will be like the Most High. . . . Thou shalt be brought down to the Pit." [35] A culture makes its possessors, and particularly its inheritors, feel superior; and at that moment the culture begins to decay. Its art becomes pretentious and trivial, its science loses keenness and energy, its politics and industry are sapped of vital force. The antidote to egotism is the vision of God, high and lifted up. This is not to urge religion as a utility to be cultivated for practical results. Whenever God is sought for anything but His own sake, religion is debased into magic. But fellowship with One above man at his loftiest, a fellowship abasing man with a sense of his inadequacy and guiltiness, detaches him from his civilization, renders sensitive his conscience to the blemishes in all its achievements, and furnishes him with an access of moral energy. It is God towering above man so that he never dreams of exalting himself or boasting in his own might, God whose holy love shames him and keeps him chastened and penitent, God whose far-reaching interests and incalculable resources transcend man's reason and imagination, who alone produces in him humility and confidence. And without these no civilization will advance and endure.

And our confidence is not in ourselves or in our civilization. We are creatures of a brief day in the earth and our civilization may even now be completing its epoch in human history. We ourselves are doubtless incompetent to assess its state as crescent or decadent. But our confidence is in God who is *more* than is discoverable in the present world. He, therefore, can out of His infinite resources renew and enrich it, or, if needs be, bring it to naught and replace it with another civilization fitter for His purpose. It is for those whose sole trust is in Him humbly and obediently to wait upon His will. Whether at any moment in history He manifests Himself in judgment or in mercy, both we believe will reveal His love embodied in Jesus Christ.

Chapter III

BIBLICAL CRITICISM

A THIRD disturber of the minds of devout Christians of Yesterday were the new ideas about the Bible, which had originated earlier in the century in Germany, and became the dominant issue in the churches here in the eighties and nineties.

The Bible had been generally regarded as throughout the inspired Word of God, and therefore without admixture of human error. It was taken literally by the mass of church people. Dr. Parkhurst has told how his farmer-schoolmaster father used to say decisively: "God began the world Monday and finished it Saturday." [1] Allowing for an inaccuracy in the good man's identification of the days of the week in the First Chapter in Genesis, his literalness is patent. Dr. Gladden has recorded a meeting of intelligent New England clergymen in Springfield, Massachusetts, in 1875, where the question arose whether it would be judicious for them to tell their people that the seventh verse of the fifth chapter of the First Epistle of John was not in the earliest manuscripts, but was probably an interpolation. Not one of the other twenty parsons agreed with him that this fact could be safely stated.[2] When the Revised Version of the New Testament appeared, six years later, and James Gordon Bennett had it cabled word by word and published it in the New York *Herald,* it was seen that this verse was omitted.

The fact of a revised translation of the Scriptures troubled some who had come to attach sanctity to the very words of the King James Version. Dr. Henry Preserved Smith, a commissioner that year at the General Assembly of the Presbyterian Church, when copies of the new version were on sale, reports a prominent pastor as exclaiming:

Revision! I am sick of the word. It has put the stamp of doubt on some of the most precious passages of the Word of God.[3]

This attitude evidenced the little interest in accurate Biblical scholarship among ministers too engrossed in the practical work of their churches. Such men were not keeping abreast of the theological movements going on at the time in Britain.

That same year (1881) the Trustees of Andover Seminary invited Dr. Newman Smyth to become professor of theology in succession to Dr. Edwards A. Park, the last rigid adherent of the old New England theology. Dr. Smyth in an address to a group of men in his church in Illinois had suggested that the heathen who died without ever having a chance to hear of Christ might have an opportunity after death. This was labeled "second probation," and was violently combatted by the leaders of the American Board on the ground that it "cut the nerve of missions." The dispute plunged the Seminary into a conflict between Trustees and Visitors—a Board charged with watching its orthodoxy—and Dr. Smyth withdrew.[4] Other members of the Andover faculty later published a series of articles under the caption *Progressive Orthodoxy.* This led to a heresy trial in Boston of five of them, in which one of the charges was that the Bible for them was "fallible and untrustworthy even in some of its religious teaching." The case dragged on for several years, creating much public discussion, and was finally settled by an appeal to the Supreme Judicial Council of Massachusetts in 1891, which reversed the decision of the Andover Board of Visitors removing one of the professors from his chair; and the next year, the Board of Visitors itself, whose personnel had changed, dismissed the whole matter.[5]

The question, however, *In what sense is the Bible authoritative?* came up clearly in connection with the trial in 1891 of Professor Charles Augustus Briggs of Union Theological Seminary in New York.

Dr. Briggs had studied in Germany, had taught for seventeen years, and was an internationally known exponent of the Bible. He had published in 1883 a volume entitled *Bible Study, Its Principles, Methods, and History,* which set forth the newer views of the Biblical documents. This book had provoked unfavorable comment from conservatives, but the public attention at the time was centered on the controversy over Evolution, and no ecclesiastical action was taken. When, however, in 1890 the Directors of Union Seminary transferred Dr. Briggs to a newly founded chair of Biblical theology, and in January, 1891, he delivered an inaugural address stating plainly the historical-critical methods of interpreting the Bible, a furious opposition broke out.

Many were shocked to be told that the traditional authorship of a number of the books was unfounded. This seemed to them to rob them of divine authority. One of Dr. Briggs' colleagues in the faculty, the venerable Dr. W. G. T. Shedd, wrote:

If . . . "the great mass of the Old Testament was written by authors whose names are lost in oblivion," it was written by uninspired men. . . . This would be the inspiration of indefinite persons like Tom, Dick, and Harry, whom nobody knows, and not of definite historical persons like Moses and David, Matthew and John, chosen by God by name and known to men.[6]

To which Dr. Briggs answered:

> Dr. Shedd cannot name the author of *The Epistle
> to the Hebrews* or of *The Book of Job*. Logically he
> should cast these out of his Bible. Does he believe
> that David wrote the whole Psalter, or that Solomon
> wrote all of the *Proverbs?* If not, what will he do with
> the orphan Psalms and the anonymous sentences of
> Wisdom, written by unknown inspired men, whom he
> calls Tom, Dick, and Harry? This dogmatic theory,
> which is pure speculation, and without basis in the
> Bible, history, or logic, is more perilous to the Bible
> than all that Baur, Kuenen, or Wellhausen have ever
> said.[7]

But the more serious shock came from Dr. Briggs'
attack upon the conception of the verbal inerrancy
of the Bible. This doctrine was the citadel of the
conservative theologians. Two of the faculty of
Princeton Seminary, Professors A. A. Hodge and
B. W. Warfield, had declared:

> A proved error in Scripture contradicts not only our
> doctrine, but the Scripture's claims, and therefore its
> inspiration in making these claims.[8]

All admitted that our present manuscripts disclose
errors; but the contenders for inerrancy insisted that
the original manuscripts, as they came from the
hands of their authors, had been so controlled in

their composition by the Spirit of God that they were without mistake. Inasmuch as no one hoped to recover these originals, the positing of inerrancy in them was like the nursery rhyme:

> Oats, peas, beans and barley grows
> Where you, nor I, nor nobody knows.

Dr. Briggs replied to such opponents:

It is not a pleasant task to point out errors in the Sacred Scriptures. . . . The errors are in the only texts we have and every one is forced to recognize them. It would be no more difficult to distinguish between the essential and the circumstantial in the *original* text, if we could in any way secure it, than it is in the texts we now have.[9]

He pointed out that inerrancy had not been the doctrine held by either the leading Reformation divines or their successors:

If the Reformers and Puritans, the great Biblical scholars of the past, have maintained their faith in the Bible notwithstanding the errors they have seen in it, it is improbable that the Biblical critics of our day will be disturbed by them. If anyone is disturbed, it will be those who have been misled by the dogmaticians to rest their faith on the doctrine of inerrancy. These will ere long find the doctrine a broken reed that will give them a severe fall and shock in their faith, if it does not pierce them to the heart with the bitter agony of perplexity and doubt.[10]

But the General Assembly of the Presbyterian Church, which had been given a veto over the election of professors at Union, proceeded to rule on a technicality that a transfer from one chair to another constituted a new election, and vetoed the appointment. Meanwhile a trial for heresy was under way before the Presbytery of New York, in which Dr. Briggs was acquitted. An appeal was taken to the General Assembly, disregarding Presbyterian law which made the Synod of New York the next court of jurisdiction, but an emotional crusade in defense of the Bible was in full swing, and the Assembly took jurisdiction, tried Dr. Briggs, condemned him, and suspended him from the ministry. The directors of the Seminary resumed an earlier independence of any "ecclesiastical domination" in which the Seminary had been founded, and Dr. Briggs was kept in his chair.[11]

But the attack on those who held the newer views about the Bible continued and spread to most of the churches. Sometimes the language and methods of the defenders of tradition passed all bounds of Christian charity; sometimes their logic was absurd. When Professor Henry Preserved Smith was tried in Cincinnati, he says of the prosecuting committee:

Their most astonishing statement was that only an

72

inerrant Scripture can have power to accomplish in the human soul the work for which the revelation has been given; that is, the work of conversion and regeneration. Since by their emphasis on the original autographs the committee conceded that there are errors in the present text, they virtually confessed that our present Bible has lost the power of converting sinners.[12]

Toward the turn of the century the controversy shifted from the Old Testament to the New. Some scholars—and Dr. Briggs among them[13]—who used the methods of historical criticism freely in handling the Old Testament, were unwilling to allow a like freedom with the Gospels. In England, Bishop Gore, who had been under attack in the previous decade for an essay in *Lux Mundi*, which set limits to our Lord's knowledge, so that when he cited an Old Testament passage as by Moses or David, such attributions of authorship could not be taken as authoritative, wished severe measures instituted in the cases of clergymen who questioned the literal interpretation of events mentioned in the creeds.[14] In this country the Congregationalists dropped Professor George H. Gilbert at Chicago Theological Seminary,[15] the Board of Bishops of the Methodist Episcopal Church refused to confirm a reappointment of Professor Hinckley G. Mitchell at Boston University,[16] the Episcopalians deposed from the ministry

73

the Rev. Algernon S. Crapsey,[17] and there were other prosecutions. In the Roman Catholic Church the Bull against Modernists was enforced, and some scholars were deprived of teaching posts and sent to minor parochial duties.

For those who accepted the results of the historical criticism the Bible assumed a new meaning. Instead of a book equally authoritative in all its parts, they had a record of the progressive Self-revelation of God to Israel culminating in Jesus and the founding of the Church, and they read the Old Testament through Christian eyes. Instead of a verbally inerrant record, they had a collection of books of various literary form by fallible men with the views of their day which told for purposes of religious edification of God's dealings with a nation and individuals and of His coming in Jesus Christ. This Book became, when read under the guidance of the Spirit of Christ, the contemporary Word of God to them for their faith and conduct.

One result of the historical interpretation of the Scriptures by Christian scholars was to render irrelevant many of the assaults by infidels which had caused much excitement and upset believers when the Bible was read as equally authoritative in all its books and verbally without mistake. Chief among these militant assailants in this country was Colonel Robert G. Ingersoll.

His stock in trade was the unscientific account of creation in the Bible, the theologic Adam, the immorality of the patriarchs, the wars and cruelties of the Israelites, the story of Jonah; attacks on certain articles in the creeds and on the theory that the Bible is absolutely free from errors; that if any page of the Scriptures is blemished, Christianity itself goes down.[18]

When leading Christian teachers admitted discrepancies between accounts of the same event in different books, that Bible writers held the scientific and ethical opinions of their time, and that they give us the record of the developing Self-disclosure of God, the ground was cut from under the feet of these assailants.

The controversy among Christians over the historical treatment of the Bible, however, broke out afresh after the Great War, and led to the movement known as Fundamentalism. One of its champions, Professor Machen, declared that he felt closer kinship with Roman Catholics who appeal to the principle of dogmatic authority than with Protestants of the modernist variety who dissent from it.[19] The most dramatic clash, which attracted world-wide notice, was the trial of a schoolteacher at Dayton, Ten-

nessee, charged with teaching Evolution in contradiction to the literal interpretation of the creation
narrative in *Genesis*—a trial where W. J. Bryan and
Clarence Darrow crossed swords as opposing counsel. Fundamentalists are still numerous and militant in many parts of the country.

It was natural that more attention should be given
to the result of the historical-critical methods in the
study of the Gospels. In the latter years of the
Nineteenth Century there were numerous Lives of
Christ, which attempted to describe Him against the
background of His time. Those by Farrar, Eder-
sheim, and Stalker had perhaps the widest circulation among Church people. These were critically
conserative, but they served to make Jesus a very real
human being. Throughout this period much work
was done by archaeologists in exploring Palestine and
neighboring lands. They supplied the background
of the Biblical narratives and enabled men to read
them in their historical setting. Numbers of papyri
were discovered, and from them it became evident
that a common language prevailed in commercial
circles about the Mediterranean. This language—
the *Koine*—helped to explain many expressions in
the New Testament. It may be said that the Christians of Yesterday had a more vivid picture of the
Man of Nazareth and Calvary in their minds and

hearts than those of any preceding century after the First.

It had been the custom to look at Jesus through the dogmatic definitions of the creeds. For example, in 1888 Professor Shedd had written:

Jesus Christ as a theanthropic person was constituted of a divine nature and a human nature. . . . The experiences of the divine nature were as diverse from those of the human nature as those of the human mind are from those of the human body. Yet there was but one person who was the subject-ego of both of these experiences. At the very time that Christ was conscious of weariness and thirst by the well of Samaria, He also was conscious that He was the eternal and only-begotten Son of God, the second person in the Trinity.[20]

In the interest of portraying Him as a genuine historical character so unquestionably orthodox and learned a divine as the then Chancellor of New York University, Dr. Howard Crosby, asserted:

Omniscience could not have been exercised by the Jesus who was growing in wisdom. If any say here, as we usually do, that the humanity grew but the divinity was omniscient, let us ask if there were two persons in Jesus.[21]

A popular doctrine was the *Kenosis* or Self-emptying—that in becoming Man the Son of God laid aside all attributes incompatible with Humanity. It was a poor doctrine, for it meant that in Jesus the Divine was not fully revealed; it was largely left behind in heaven. But it remains in the teaching of many ministers.

With the use of the methods of historical investigation it became customary in portraying Jesus to start with a normal human figure. Dr. Rainsford is typical of hundreds of his contemporaries among Christian teachers, when he wrote:

Jesus was realest of the real. He shared the beliefs of His time. He believed in the nearness of the parousia—as did Paul—and was mistaken. He was under *all* the conditions not only of humanity, but of the humanity of His time and place. So much was essential to a true incarnation. Incarnation meant conditions. He did not know any more about philosophy or philology, about history or natural laws, than did any Jew about Him, *except in so far as a pure heart helps knowledge.*

The more convincedly we believe in the *Incarnation,* the more strongly must we hold to the conditions and limitations of it; without them the Incarnation is not real. Where, then, is the Divineness? It is in the perfection of His obedience, and the resulting absoluteness of His moral and spiritual verdicts.[22]

Dr. George Harris, professor of theology at Andover, later president of Amherst, summed up the result of the historical treatment of the Gospels:

78

We have recovered the humanity of Jesus, and know Him the God-filled Man.[23]

Critical scholars who wrote reconstructions of the figure of Jesus taught that He spiritualized the realistic Messianic expectations of contemporary Judaism; that He conceived His Messianic role to be that of the Founder and Teacher of the kingdom of God; and that, when He was misunderstood and rejected, He resolved to die for His cause and thus carry it to victory. Jesus was modernized, and made acceptable to Nineteenth-Century minds. Then Johannes Weiss, and later Albert Schweitzer, upset this interpretation which fitted Jesus so smoothly into the current view of the world. Schweitzer insisted:

For the historical understanding of the life of Jesus it is necessary to think out all the consequences of the fact that He did actually live in the eschatological, Messianic thought-world of late Judaism, and try to comprehend His resolutions and actions, not by means of considerations drawn from psychology, but solely by motives provided by His eschatological expectations.[24]

Here was a Figure not so easily adapted to the prevalent immanentist view of God—a Jesus who believed in a God above and invading the world, and whose Messiah was a supernatural Being in whom God entered it in judgment to redeem it and

79

establish His reign. To some it made Jesus more remote and unintelligible; it prepared the way for a new appraisal which was to be made later.

Meanwhile another and kindred factor affecting the religious outlook of the men of Yesterday had been at work. The same historical methods which had been applied in the study of Hebrew and Christian religion were used in the investigation of other faiths. These had been lumped together in Christian minds under the caption "heathen religions." It was now seen that religion, like man himself, had undergone a long evolution, and had taken many forms, some lower and some loftier in ethical content. The lines (probably too undiscriminating and over-generous) of Matthew Arnold expressed the views of many Christians:

Children of men! the unseen Power, whose eye
　Forever doth accompany mankind,
Hath look'd on no religion scornfully
　That men did ever find.

Which has not taught weak wills how much they can?
　Which has not fall'n on the dry heart like rain?
Which has not cried to sunk, self-weary man:
　Thou must be born again!

A Parliament of Religions was held in connection with the World's Fair in Chicago in 1893, and attracted wide attention. It was apparent that in their rituals, theologies, and institutions religions often showed striking similarities. Some scholars emphasized the borrowings of Israel and even of St. Paul from the rites and conceptions of other faiths. Books like Sir James Frazer's *Golden Bough* [25] were read by intellectuals and their contents seeped gradually down to the public mind. It was puzzling to discover that other faiths had trinities and virgin births and sacramental meals, which had been associated only with the revealed Christian religion. After some years of discussion it became patent that whatever likenesses there might be in externals, in its basic conviction of the character of God as Christlike love, with all that this implied, Christianity stood alone. The other faiths were now regarded not as false religions to be combatted, but as stages in the development of man's fellowship with God. There were, doubtless, falsities in them and many childishnesses to be outgrown. Christians viewed the Gospel of Christ as the consummation of this fellowship. It was not *a* religion beside others, but *religion*—the complete communion of God with men. This sent missionaries out not to destroy, but to fulfill.

One unhappy effect of the newer views of the Bible, coupled with the stress on man's activity in religion (to which allusion has been made in an earlier lecture), was to push into the background the conception of Revelation. The Bible was spoken of as the record of man's developing religious experience, rather than as God's word to His children. God was presented as an undiscovered continent inertly waiting for man's adventurous exploration. Jesus was pictured as the Pioneer who went farthest in reaching God and opening up spiritual resources for Himself and His brethren. God's initiative in the intercourse between earth and heaven was lost sight of. One heard little in liberal circles of either Revelation or Incarnation, but much of the quest for the Divine and of the leadership of Jesus in that quest. To be sure, there is no revelation without man's response to God's approach, and the Incarnation of God in the Man of Nazareth involved His growth in fellowship with His Father, His struggle with doubt and temptation, His education through suffering into power to redeem. But the spiritual attainments of the saints and of the Son of God had their origin in the Most High Himself, who spoke to listening men and who sent His Son. The earlier exponents of Biblical criticism, with a different background, were careful to insist on God's Self-revelation. They stressed the priority of God in making Himself known and supremely in His Self-embodiment in Jesus. Dr. William J. Tucker, another Andover professor, later president of Dartmouth, said:

To my mind the person of Christ represents God revealed, not God attained.[26]

But some of the later exponents of the historical-critical position reversed this emphasis. A popular preacher in the Post-War years published a series of sermons under the title: *The Man Who Dared to Be God.*[27]

Another unforeseen sequel to this movement, for which it was certainly not mainly responsible, but which it did not prevent, was the widespread ignorance of the contents of the Bible. Americans of the older stock had been accustomed to hear the Bible in family worship daily and in their church services. Many of them read it faithfully. The newer Americans had not this background, and the habit of family worship rapidly disappeared in the 1880's and 1890's. The religious educators who came to the fore, particularly in the years immediately following the War, did not make the Bible the center of the curriculum which they advised. The earlier Biblical critics had expected that the Bible, freed from the dogmatic presuppositions which seemed to them to conceal its meaning and to raise obstacles to the appreciation of its faith, would be much more widely read and its teaching understood. The Bible would become the instrument by which they saw life in the light of the invisible God. As light is known and prized because of what it enables us to see—the world in its richness and beauty, so revelation in this Book is known and valued because of what it reveals—God and the world and mankind of and in and under Him.

Dr. William Newton Clarke concludes an autobiographical volume on *Sixty Years:*

By this time in the history of the world (1909) the quality of the Bible as the book of divine religion is so established that we may think of it with serene confidence. . . . Our sacred book is our guide to Jesus, to God, and to life divine. This fact has been established in long human experience, and can be trusted.[28]

When I viewed the Bible as a body of statements, it was natural that I should use it chiefly as an *object* of study. I was seeking to know what the statements meant. When I came to view it as an expression of principles, the principles of divine religion, it thereby became to me a *means* of study: then I sought to know whither the principles led. The book thus became to me an instrument of advance, an opportunity for the obtaining of further light upon the matters of which it treats. The significance of these last years is that in them I have more and more used the Bible as the divine guide and inspiration for my own study of the things of God.[29]

But the task of teachers of the Bible is still largely incomplete. No doubt there is to be progress in understanding the contents of the Scriptures themselves; but the main task is to induce men to become familiar with the Bible and let it throw its light upon the confused world about them, upon their own divinely given duty and upon the unseen Father and Lord who opens to them the fullness of life with Him. When read by the Spirit of Christ, Christians still hear God speaking personally to them through its pages. It contains for the Church the abiding Word of God, the authoritative standard of faith and life.

With regard to the New Testament and the portraits which it furnishes us of Jesus Christ, this is not the occasion (nor is the present lecturer competent) to list in detail the changes which the more than thirty years since the appearance of Schweitzer's book have wrought. The effort has been made to go behind our sources and reach the oral tradition by discovering the forms in which the doings and sayings of Jesus were presented in missionary preaching and in sermons to Christian congregations. It has also been tried to discern the probable Aramaic form of the sayings of Jesus. These attempts may have brought us a step nearer the earliest tradition. It has become plain, however, that the Christ in whom Christians have trusted, and through whom they have found God coming to them, has not been some historic figure reconstructed by a critical scholar; but the Christ of the New Testament. Further Christians have not felt themselves before one Christ in the Synoptic Gospels and before another Christ in St. John or in the epistles of St. Paul. There are differences in the various portraits which the writers give us; but amid the differences there is a unity of religious impression. It is the same life-giving Christ who confronts us in them all. And this is the Christ whom the Church of all the Christian centuries has worshiped and preached.

The careful historical and critical study of the documents is not to be disparaged. Every shade of thought and every changing need in the early Church which would color any writer's presentation of the figure of Jesus must be considered. But the general result of New Testament investigation appears to be that for purposes of religion—and these are the sole purposes for which the books were written and preserved—we have a trustworthy portrayal of the Jesus who lived and taught, died and rose again—a reliable record of the impression His personality made upon those who knew and believed in Him at the first, and in the immediately following generations. In the words of my former colleague,

Professor Ernest F. Scott, it may be given as the mature judgment of a lifelong scholar of the New Testament:

> For our knowledge of Jesus we must indeed depend on the records, left to us by those primitive teachers who alone had acquaintance with the facts. Yet we can be certain that they witnessed truly, for their religion was one with the history. They believed that God had revealed Himself through Jesus Christ, and for that belief they willingly died. But the revelation had no meaning for them apart from the actual life. They recorded the life with the full consciousness that if Jesus had not lived in this manner their faith was vain. It was in the facts that God had spoken, and by the knowledge of them men would apprehend God. This is our ultimate security for the Gospel record.[30]

The insistence upon the *otherness* of God—His transcendence of the world and His unlikeness to man—which characterizes the thought of our day has affected the view held of Christ. To the immanentist Jesus is the instance of the Man unbrokenly conscious of God, at one with Him in purpose and fully sharing His life. His origin seems unimportant, and His oneness with the Father is represented as His own moral achievement. But when God is thought of as over against, as well as invading, the world of history, Jesus appears the chief instance of God's entrance into it. This Man is uniquely from God and in Him God has come. Some go so far in their stress on the difference between God and man that they represent the figure of the historic Jesus merely as an *incognito*. It is not His personality in whom God is seen; behind the human personality faith apprehends the Person of Christ, who alone is divine. But this almost destroys the Incarnation—God revealing Himself in the Man Christ Jesus. A saner position has been taken by a Cambridge scholar, Professor Creed:

> Revelation is not so much Revelation of a supernatural otherwise wholly unknown, but rather a Way which enables man to relate himself aright to the whole universe with which he is in contact—physical, moral, religious—in the light of a Person accepted by faith as ultimate and supreme.[31]

The historic Jesus, who lived, taught, suffered, and triumphed, and whose impression on the faith of His first followers is preserved for us in the New Testament, is to the Church the authoritative disclosure of the living God. Whoever sees Him with trust and loyalty sees the Father.

In a previous lecture it has been pointed out that we no longer view the immanent God in the ethical trends of our time; but think of Him above and often in contrast to them—their Judge and would-be Transformer. This renders it the more imperative for Christians to ask: Where does God make Himself authentically known? Our answer is nearer the answer of an earlier day than that of our immediate predecessors. We recognize with the New Testament that God has not left Himself anywhere without witness, that He has always been seeking and speaking to men as they were able to hear Him. But for us His complete Self-unveiling is in Christ, and is recorded in the Scriptures which interpret the events leading up to His advent and issuing from it in the founding of the Church. There is therefore a new emphasis upon Christ and the Bible.

This should restore the Scriptures to the central place in religious education and in the preaching of the pulpit. We have suffered from vague talk of religious experience. History has been disparaged by ultra-modern Americans, who had the conceit that they could discard the past and start afresh. A leader in religious education has contrasted transmissive and creative education:

The Christian teacher's practical dilemma takes this form: Shall the primary purpose of Christian education be to hand on a religion, or to create a new world? [32]

It is a false dilemma. Christianity is an historic

faith.   Its God is the God of Abraham, Isaac, and
Jacob, the God of the prophets, above all the God
and Father of the Lord Jesus Christ.   He has revealed Himself most significantly for man's redemption and the creation of a new society in certain
events of the past, of which the Scriptures, put together and treasured by the Church, are the life-
transmitting record.   He is revealing Himself today, but not as One other than He showed Himself
in Christ.   Jesus, therefore, permanently defines
God for us, although we are not confined to the disclosure of God in Him.   There must be a constant
transmission of the heritage in the Christian classic
if each new generation is to be possessed by the creative Spirit who wrought in the seers of Israel and in
the Son of God.   The Christian Church has its
normative and authoritative Word of God given in
the Bible read in the light of Jesus Christ.

Chapter IV

RELIGIOUS EXPERIENCE

In our Yesterday much was said of religious experience. This, of course, was not an altogether novel emphasis. It is found in many epochs of the Church's history, notably in Pietism and in the Evangelical Revival of the Eighteenth Century, and it was basic in the theology of Schleiermacher, who together with Ritschl dominated the progressive theological thinking of the Nineteenth Century. But American Christians, reared in the belief in an inerrant Bible as the impregnable foundation of their faith, when that was shaken by historical inquiry, fell back upon their own consciousness of God. In 1890, just a year before the delivery of Dr. Briggs' inaugural address in the same Seminary in New York City, Professor Lewis F. Stearns of Bangor delivered a notable series of lectures on *The Evidence of Christian Experience.*

"It does not meet the demand of the time," he said, "to prove the truth of Christianity as a mere system of doctrine; what men need most to know is that it is the living, present, perennial power of God, by which He is redeeming the world." [1]

This evidence was found in what God had done and was doing to change individuals and society. The head of a very useful philanthropic organization published a widely read book captioned *Gesta Christi* [2]—the work of Christ through the centuries and in the present for human betterment. A leader in the propaganda of the Gospel compiled three volumes on *Christian Missions and Social Progress*.[3] The Christians of Yesterday confidently appealed to its fruits as the cogent argument for God's presence in the Gospel of Christ.

But Dr. Stearns chiefly concerned himself with

the manifestation to the believer himself, in his own inward spiritual life, of the presence and power of God and the Christian realities.[4]

Accepting the current evolutionary science, he did not share the prevailing opinion that evil was good in the making. He quotes with relish the witty thrust at the evolutionist who does not exclaim with Paul, "O wretched man that I am! who shall deliver me?" but "O progressive creature that I am! who shall help me to evolve myself?" [5] Christian experience is for him redemption from sin and advance into Christian character and service. And

The new life in its beginning and its growth contains the proof of its own reality and divinity.[6]

Nor is this an individual experience; it is the experience of the Christian Church in all its branches and in all the centuries. And a characteristic of the Christian's assurance is that as time goes on his certainty

enlarges and deepens, and he more and more verifies by actual contact the contents of the notions furnished by the Gospel.[7]

Dr. Stearns' argument assumes that God has revealed Himself in a unique way in a series of historical events which reached their climax in the coming of Jesus Christ and the founding of the Church, that He has given an interpretation of these events by the prophets and in the teaching of His Son and His apostles, and that by His Spirit He has been and is now present and working to carry out this redemption of mankind. Those who respond to His approach discover in the results within themselves and their fellow-Christians the power and truth of the Gospel. This is a convincing verification of their faith in their own experience.

Psychology was at that time a most popular science, and nowhere more so than in this country, and its exponents were making vast strides in exploring human nature. The current emphasis upon religion as experience interested them, and they commenced to investigate and classify the religious life of their devout contemporaries. The most distinguished of these psychological investigators of religion was William James, who gave his results in his Gifford Lectures for 1902 on *The Varieties of Religious Experience*. He had, however, been preceded by one of his own pupils, Dr. Edward D. Starbuck, who had collected a vast amount of material from believing Christians in answer to a series of questionnaires.[8]

At first the devout were shocked to have the sacred secret places of the soul invaded by prying explorers. But on second thought it was reassuring that their religious experiences were taken seriously by respected men of science. In his preface to Dr. Starbuck's *The Psychology of Religion*, Professor James wrote:

Rightly interpreted, the whole tendency of Dr. Starbuck's patient labor is to bring compromise and conciliation into the long-standing feud of Science and Religion. Your "evangelical" extremist will have it that conversion is an absolutely supernatural event, with nothing cognate to it in ordinary psychology. Your "scientist" sectary, on the other hand, sees nothing in it but hysterics and emotionalism, an absolutely pernicious pathological disturbance. For Dr. Starbuck, it is neither of these things. It may in countless cases be a perfectly normal psychologic crisis, marking the transition from the child's world to the wider world of youth, or from that of youth to that of maturity—a crisis which the evangelical machinery only methodically emphasises, abridges, and regulates.[9]

These sympathetic inquiries into the inner lives of Christians added this uncharted spiritual realm to those in which known laws exist. There are discoverable principles in the responses of souls to religious stimuli; there are more and less impressionable stages in their careers; there are periods when changes are to be expected. Further there are types of religious experience which can be distinguished and classified. These investigations threw light upon the distinctive features of the religious life of childhood, of adolescence, of maturity, upon the difficulties encountered in passing from one stage to another in spiritual development, upon doubt and its causes and cure, upon losing and regaining the sense of fellowship with God, upon growth or deterioration in conviction and character. These explorers of the Christian experience were for the most part moved not merely by scientific curiosity; they were eager to assist the Church to deal more wisely with young and old, to avoid mistakes in her training and her evangelism, and to be more skillful in winning and holding disciples of Christ and in developing in them His mind. As a result there were changes in methods of religious education and in missionary effort, and pastors learned much for their counseling of their people. Psychologists rightly insisted on the "varieties" of religious experience, upon the necessity of discriminating between wholesome and unwholesome forms, upon the impossibility of forcing souls into a single pattern of devout life, upon the urgency of adapting the Church's worship and education and social activities to the diverse needs of folk, younger and older. One has only to glance over the numbers of books produced under the stimulus of this new study of Christian experience to see how widespread an interest was awakened and how large an influence was exercised upon every phase of the Church's life and work.

The classification of religious experience which attracted most attention, then as now, was that by Professor James, when he divided the devout into the once- and the twice-born, or into "the healthy-minded" and "the sick souls." The former were optimists who either denied the existence of evil or felt man competent to overcome it; the latter were pessimists who regarded the world and themselves in the grip of a sinister enslaving tyranny and desperate unless God came to their deliverance. Their world "is a double-storied mystery" [10] and the help which comes to their rescue from above turns their despair into hope. In his Gifford Lectures he preferred the sick souls as the profounder type of believer; but in a later series of lectures he praised the former as more apt to see their God Himself embroiled and struggling against iniquity and likelier to enlist as His comrades in the battle.[11] This pragmatic view of God and of the life with Him fitted in with the popular thought of that day in this country.

We have already spoken of the stress on man's active role in the religious life. Professor James gave classic expression to this in the title of an address delivered at Yale in 1896, *The Will to Believe*. It was man, rather than God, who took the initiative In his later works he spoke of the "faith-ladder," and made plain that it is man who erects it:

A conception of the world arises in you somehow, no matter how. Is it true or not? you ask.

It *might* be true, somewhere, you say, for it is not self-contradictory.

It *may* be true, you continue, even here and now.

It is *fit* to be true, it would be *well if it were true;* it *ought* to be true, you presently feel.

It *must* be true, something persuasive in you whispers next; and then—as a final result—

It shall be *held for true,* you decide; it *shall be* as if true, for *you.*[12]

Here is a faith which stands in the power of man.

In an age which concerned itself particularly with origins, it was inevitable that there should be much inquiry into the birth of religion. Anthropologists reported its presence everywhere, even among the most primitive peoples. Its universality led many to ascribe it to a particular faculty in human nature,[13] to an instinct as fundamental as gregariousness or sex or hunger. Some spoke of faith as "a sixth sense." [14] In revolt against the intellectualism of orthodox theology which had made revealed truth the primary source of the devout life, most psychologists made prerational feeling the main element in religious experience. They were apt to disparage both the institutions and the creeds which enshrined the faith. These were secondary—mere temporary creations of religious feeling. It was common to speak of "abiding experiences" and the "changing forms" in which these expressed themselves.

There was a difference of opinion whether the religious experience was something entirely distinctive. The scholar who did most to try to establish its unique character was Professor Rudolf Otto. He believed that the experience was a complicated affair in which subrational and rational and ethical elements combine. His chief book bears the title *The Holy* (*Das Heilige,* Englished not quite accurately *The Idea of the Holy*), with the subtitle:

"An inquiry into the non-rational factor in the idea of the divine and its relation to the rational." For this non-rational element he coined the term *numinous:*

I shall speak . . . of a definitely "numinous" state of mind. . . . This mental state is perfectly *sui generis* and irreducible to any other; and therefore, like every absolutely primary and elementary datum, while it admits of being discussed, it cannot be strictly defined. . . . It can only be evoked, awakened in the mind, as everything that comes "of the spirit" must be awakened.[15]

In the believing soul this is "creature feeling"—

the emotion of a creature submerged and overwhelmed by its own nothingness in contrast to that which is supreme above all creatures.[16]

What is experienced is a Mystery, both awesome and fascinating.

The truly "mysterious" object is beyond our apprehension and comprehension, not only because our knowledge has certain irremovable limits, but because in it we come upon something "wholly other," whose kind and character are incommensurable with our own, and before which we therefore recoil in a wonder that strikes us chill and numb.[17]

99

Otto was eager, as he tells us in an earlier book, to "vindicate against the counter-claims of naturalism the validity and freedom of the religious outlook." [18] The religious experience having its unique quality in this infra-rational numinous feeling stands in its own right. It is not to be expected that the beliefs in which it utters itself will be entirely congruous with man's scientific views. Religious conceptions

weave themselves together out of the most inward and subtle experiences, out of impressions which are coarsened in the very act of expressing them. Their import and value must be judged entirely by the standards of conscience and feeling, by their own self-sufficiency and validity. [19]

Most American scholars have followed James in believing in the "varieties" of religious experience, rather than in finding its distinctive quality in this numinous feeling, although Otto has made a permanently valuable contribution to its analysis.

All of them, Otto included, have noted psychological similarities in the experiences of believers of many faiths. Conversion, renewal, enlightenment, the integration of the self occur in other religions than the Christian and, for that matter, in realms of life not usually labeled religious. And the finding of psychologically common elements in various faiths brought the conclusion that the stuff of religious experience was the same everywhere, however its theological interpretations might differ. An often repeated saying of a generation ago ran: "Religions are many, religion is one." This assisted tolerance, and led to the combination of devout people of widely varying traditions and beliefs for practical efforts.

In that scientific and materialistic day, when believers felt hard put to it to justify their faith, and a typical book bore the significant title, *The Seeming Unreality of the Spiritual Life*,[20] it was reassuring to be told that those who explored with rigorous scholarly methods the experiences of religious men and women arrived at the conclusion that they were not deluded. Professor Otto quotes with approval a saying of Professor James:

It is as if there were in the human consciousness *a sense of reality, a feeling of objective presence, a perception of* what we may call *"something there,"* more deep and more general than any of the special "senses" by which the current psychology supposes existent realities to be originally revealed.[21]

The underlying agreements discovered in the lives of religious people were all the more significant because their creeds and rituals were often so opposed and different. They witnessed to the actuality of the spiritual world. Men felt with Professor James that they could not "poohpooh" God away.[22] He wrote to Professor Starbuck that a chief aim of his Gifford Lectures was

to make the hearer or reader believe, what I myself invincibly do believe, that, although all the special manifestations of religion may have been absurd (I mean its creeds and theories), yet the life of it as a whole is mankind's most important function.[23]

In that James was repeating the faith of a British scientist of an earlier day who is said to have written in a private letter:

Old Chap! I have read up many queer religions; there is nothing like the old thing after all. I have looked into most philosophical systems, and I have seen that none will work without God.[24]

The assurance of the spiritual Fact which such students reached is well summed up in the title of Professor H. N. Wieman's book, *Religious Experience and Scientific Method*.

This scientific treatment of religious experience had, however, a baleful consequence. To the scientist all explanations of phenomena are hypotheses—

valuable for the time being, but subject to correction, and to be discarded for better, if better be found. In student circles it became the fashion to speak of God as an hypothesis. The assured data were the religious experiences: God, up to date, appeared the most available explanation of them. But what God is like can only be conjectured from the experiences; and they were so various. Could personality be ascribed to Him? Did the "numinous" or other "mystic" feeling carry a persuasion of His moral character? If God were an hypothesis how long would this explanation be held valid? God hardly seemed to them "a rock of habitation" to which they might "continually resort." He was a mere tent of their own contriving which for the present sheltered them precariously and might go down before the next high wind of changing opinion.

Psychologists of another type from those who pioneered in investigating religious experience in our Yesterday came forward with very different interpretations of it. They termed it "wishful thinking." James' "faith-ladder" and "will to believe," wrenched from the context of his own careful thought, exposed themselves to this description. Religion was infantilism in adults who could not face the stark actualities of life, and used an "escape mechanism" from their loneliness by "projecting" a father in the sky on whom they could depend, as they had relied on human parents in a childhood which they were incapable of outgrowing. Its language was "symbolism fabricated by the unconscious to express its wish fancies." [25] These symbols or myths arose out of the cultures in which their devotees lived.

There were elements of truth in these descriptions of certain forms of religion. The false assumption was that an explanation of a psychological process did away with any genuine intercourse through it. The result was that believers, looking for immediate experience of God, became introspective, questioned their own "states of consciousness," and felt themselves confined within a subjective prison. Other generations had lost God in institutions or in creeds; ours lost Him in themselves. God was at most an "idea," an "image"; they had no assurance that they were in contact with objective reality when they prayed. The intellectual difficulties of the thoughtful in matters of personal religion during the past three decades have arisen oftenest from the realm of psychology.

There was a "theology of religious experience" (and in this the influence of Schleiermacher is clear), which further involved Christians in subjectivism. Beliefs were said to be generated by the immediate contacts with God which true believers experienced. The reflection in which the belief was thought out might introduce alien elements, but the belief was again "proved" by subsequent experience. This "proof" from religious experience appears in the verse of a familiar Gospel hymn:

> I love to tell the story,
> Because I know 'tis true;
> It satisfies my longings
> As nothing else can do.

But the individual's longings are no infallible clue to ultimate Fact. Meanings cannot be read off from experiences, nor can these meanings be validated by further repetitions of the experience. As Professor John M. Moore has recently written:

There is no justification for appealing to religious experience as the final authority in religion, save in the general sense that any religious belief or attitude must in the long run be tested by its fidelity to human experience in general.[20]

This exclusive concern with religious experience fitted in with the "Humanism" of the post-War decade, and the practical abandonment of the attempt to identify the God of personal religion with the God of nature and of history.

Today religious experience is being viewed differently. While Auguste Sabatier's often-quoted remark that "man is incurably religious" still holds, and the religious capacity is recognized as part of universal human nature, man shows his piety in a myriad forms. There is apparently no such thing as a religious instinct or attitude or feeling which is common in all religious experience. It seems wiser not to speak of "religious experience," which is a mere abstraction, but of "religious experiences." These are of varying validity and worth. When one compares the religion of a primitive tribe with that of contemporary Christians, the differences are more significant than the similarities. Each of the chief religious traditions imparts a distinctive tone and quality and direction to the feelings and attitudes which it evokes in its adherents. And within the same tradition there are wide variations in the experiences of those who employ the identical religious symbols and profess the identical loyalties.

There is a reaction from the anti-intellectualism of the last generation. It is recognized that the religious feeling, which they considered primary, is affected by antecedent beliefs—by the whole spiritual heritage out of which it springs. And there is no lofty intercourse with God in which the believer is not mentally broad awake. An unthinking experience is certainly not a religious experience. Professor John Baillie has well written:

Religion lives . . . by insight. A man is religious not in so far as he stumbles on certain new facts, but in so far as he discovers a new meaning in facts that are known to us all. And it is in this discovery, in this insight, that he comes into touch and commerce with the unseen God. Hence neither is it true to say . . . that religious belief is consequent upon religious experience, nor . . . that religious experience is consequent on a prior act of belief; the truth being rather that the deepest of all religious experiences is just the experience of believing.[27]

Beside which statement one may place the dictum of Augustine:

Everyone who believes thinks. He both thinks in believing and believes in thinking.[28]

Nor are we today stressing *unmediated* contact with God in religious experience. It may be satisfactory to the believer to possess "a sense of 'something there' "; but many genuinely religious people do not have it, and probably most religious people have it only fitfully. The lack of the sense of it is no indication that the Divine Presence is not there. Primitive animists who feel spirits, malignant and kindly, everywhere about them, or superstitious

107

persons who believe in ghosts in some "haunted house" have a terrifyingly vivid feeling of "something there," while practical Christians devotedly giving themselves in service to human need may be without this mystic awareness of God. The concern of Christianity is not with the "sense of something there," but with the character of Him who is there. It believes that His people's contact with God is immediate and continuous, for the Eternal is their Contemporary. The Church declares that her Lord is with His followers always, that His Spirit dwells and works unceasingly in and through the fellowship of believers, that her God is "a very present help." But this does not mean that the current experiences of her members supply the main revelation of the Invisible with whom they have to do. That revelation has been given, and given once for all in its fullness, in the life, death, and resurrection of Jesus Christ. This revelation is transmitted in the tradition of the Christian Church—in its Canon of Holy Scripture, in its hymns, in its prayers, in its sacraments, in its whole life. The individual Christian is the heir of this tradition, and whether he be aware of it or not, it mediates God to him. His present fellowship with God is through the historic figure of Christ, recorded in the Gospels and vital in the Church. One of Yesterday's outstanding theologians, Professor Herrmann, admirably phrased it:

That is the true presence of God in our hearts when
we experience how the tidings He gives us through
Christ place the world and our sin beneath our feet.
And this is the presence of Christ which we can *experience* in true communion with God, when His appearance in history comes home to our hearts as the
most important thing in all the world. We Christians
cannot experience any other presence of God and
Christ, and we desire no other.[29]

The investigators of religious experience in Yesterday concerned themselves too exclusively with
personal relations with God, and lost sight of the
corporate communion of the Church. They were
critical of the churches as conventional, and thought
them likely to stifle originality and to try to conform
their more intense members to their own dull and
tame patterns of feeling and action. Bergson has
drawn a suggestive distinction between closed and
open morality, and between the static and dynamic
religion which accompanies each of these types.[30]
Like his predecessors of Yesterday, he associates the
ethics and faith of the Church with the former. This
in his analysis makes the religion of the Church a
factor for the cohesiveness of the nation as against
other nations, consequently a factor for war. Nor is
it difficult to point to situations in which this has

been and still is the case. But this by no means demonstrates that the Christian Church is a producer of closed and not of open morality. Great institutions are conservative, since they pass on the spiritual inheritance and do not wish to hazard any of its accumulated gains. And they move slowly, for the most part, taxing the patience of their more ardent members, who forget the numbers of their fellow-churchmen to be kindled by a fresh enthusiasm or enlisted in and trained for a new undertaking. But their fidelity to their tradition may be the very means of holding them to an open morality—to a quality of life (such as Bergson desires) with universal sympathies and interests, and with scope in it for freedom and advance. It must never be forgotten that the Christian Church carries with her down the ages the compulsion to self-criticism in the figure of her Lord. She can never be both loyal to Him and identify her standards with any system of national or racial or class morality. Witness the struggle today between both Protestant and Roman Catholic Christians and the totalitarian state. So long as Christ remains ahead of contemporary morality (and there is no indication of its catching up with, much less of its outdistancing Him), the Church will be constrained to criticize and protest the current life of the world, and keep supplying fresh inspirations from her own fountain of renewal. Any religion in which the figure of Christ is central must be "dynamic," not "static."

No doubt all institutions tend to hold back their more progressive members, as they tend to pull forward the laggard. This is their peril and their value. A widely read spiritual leader of Yesterday, George Tyrrell, writes in one of his letters:

> The antinomy I wrestle with is that institutionalism, or externalism, is at once essential and fatal to religion. Every day I feel more of a Catholic (not Roman) and more of a Quaker than ever.[81]

The Church needs seers and saints, and even plain rebels, who disturb her complacency. And in every generation there is a conflict to make her fellowship roomy enough to include them. But even they owe far more to the community of believers, both in its encouragements and in its antagonisms to them, than they realize. And happily the Church is subject to revivals—periods when some factor in her tradition comes alive with power, and in this access of divine strength she alters the mind and conscience of a generation. Botanists and zoologists formerly studied specimens of plants and animals by themselves. Their successors are making much of ecology—the science of the habitat in which plants of various sorts and animals of various species are found in association. Their interdependence is all-important. Our day is discovering the interdependence of souls in the Church of Christ. We are recognizing how vastly much we owe to each other despite denominational barriers which historic situations and human imperfection have reared high. And we are laboring hard to remove these and enrich the Christians of tomorrow by enabling them to possess together the spiritual home God wills for them in a reunited Church.

Nor is our Day viewing religious experience as man's "quest for God." Professor James' "faith-ladder" is a revealing symbol of the state of mind of the Christians of Yesterday. They had been brought up on the assumption that God had broken silence and spoken His word to man in an inerrant Bible. When that Bible came under discussion and was viewed as the record of man's progressive experience of God, most of them ceased to think that they had a God who took the initiative. He became "a distant and wholly passive object toward which man's mind must feel its baffled way as best it can." [32] Hence the need of "the will to believe," and all the careful thinking known as "the philosophy of religion" by which it was sought to open a route along which intelligent seekers could enter upon "religious experience." But to the thoughtful of Today a God reached only at the end of a search would not be the God and Father of Jesus Christ. He has always been "long beforehand" with His children. "He first loved us." "He sent His Son." Instead of man's quest, it seems more fitting to speak of his "response." Man does not set out with a definition of what he thinks God should be and try to find Him. He assumes that God is seeking him, and his task is not to prove Him, but to identify and recognize Him along any of the various paths by which He arrives.

To be sure, religious experience is two-way traffic. It is a ladder on which angels ascend and descend. There is a double approach—God's to man and man's to God. But God's approach precedes man's and draws man. The men of Yesterday did well to insist that man could not be passive. He must, as a prophet describes it, "stir up himself to lay hold on God." [33] But his alertness is needed because God is already here and seeking to lay hold of him, and he must see and receive Him. No word has come into more frequent use than the term "the given." God is the Giver and in every experience man the recipient. And since to the Christian God has given His Son and is giving His Spirit through the Church and her heritage and fellowship, he does not go out on a voyage of discovery, but waits in expectation before Christ in the company of His people. A Christian philosophy, therefore, does not start with a variety of data in human experience and gradually push its way to distinctive Christian experience. It begins with the Christian premise—God's Self-disclosure and the consequent life of the Christian Church—and then relates what is thus "given" to the total experience of man.[34]

While we no longer speak of our beliefs as produced or proved by religious experience, this does not mean that the life of the Christian is any less an evidence both to others and to himself of the reality and presence of God. It still remains true that Christian characters are the most cogent evangelists —"living epistles" commending the faith. It is also true that to the Christian his life in and with God through Christ is the basis of his assurance that he is not the dupe of an illusion, but the possessor of the highest and most enriching of friendships. The "insider" has his own knowledge of Him who is the Home of the soul and of the satisfactions of "the household of faith." He cannot convey his appreciations adequately to "outsiders." But for himself he knows "whom he has believed" and would not part with Him for the world. His knowledge is akin to that which friends have of each other or to that of husband and wife. It began in a venture of faith; it has gone on to a settled confidence.

But in discussing this "evidence of Christian experience," it is important to ask the right questions. We do not inquire, Does God satisfy the longings of man? Usually man's longings must be completely changed. His natural desires are most in need of altering. Christ makes men over, and it is "new men" who appreciate and adore Him.

Psychological research, which rightly takes all forms of religious experience as its province, ignores in its method the distinction between the "religious experience" of the regenerate and of those who have never truly surrendered themselves to God. But this scientific method—which purports to get along without theological presuppositions—really rests upon the highly questionable theological assumption of a natural affinity between the holy God and man-just-as-he-is, so that God is accessible to man without a prior reconciliation, which man cannot establish and which he can only accept in humble repentance and faith. According to classic Christianity to have a genuine religious experience—that is, "to know God"—is possible only to those who love. Such love is "of God" and comes to those who yield themselves to Christ's re-creating control.

Nor should we ask with the moderns, Does God

adjust men to life? Here is the point at which Christian counselors part company with many psychiatrists. These seek normal adjustments to life as it is. The Christian must always be discontented with and maladjusted to life as it is. To fit into it is to be a worldling. He is an "alien" and a "pilgrim" in the earth. His adjustment is to God and to His kingdom.

Nor is it sensible to say, as many preachers do, that "Christ satisfies every need of man." Some of men's pressing current needs are economic, and they must be met by a more wisely arranged economic system. Others are political, and demand a more skillfully contrived government—local, national, and international. Others again are physical and mental difficulties, and their solutions must come from more adequate knowledge of the human body and mind. It is as ridiculous to seek answers to these questions in religion, as it would be to ask of it solutions to our problems in agriculture or cooking or engineering. But all these needs are human needs, and religion has to do with man—with man in his relation to God and the world unseen and seen, in his relations individual and corporate with fellow men. Christ claims to be the answer to the basic human problem, the Creator of a new quality of life. "I am come that they might have life, and have it more abundantly." That He produces this in those who make Him their Lord, and that through them He produces it in human society, is the indisputable fact which the world has faced again and again, and which remains the chief persuasion leading men to Him and assuring those who know Him of His inestimable worth.

Chapter V

The Social Conscience

THE decades which followed the Civil War witnessed a growth of wealth in this country perhaps unrivaled in history. Railroads spanned the continent from the Atlantic to the Pacific; new lands were constantly opened for settlement and brought under cultivation; mining boomed; petroleum discovered in Pennsylvania on the eve of the War became a major product, and by the nineties the wells were yielding a hundred million barrels of oil a year. Steel grew from an infant to a mammoth industry. Immigrants by the hundred thousand, and then by the million, a year streamed across the ocean, packed in the steerage of the ever speedier "greyhounds" to supply manual labor for farm and furnace, factory and mine, and domestic service. It was the epoch of the "almighty dollar"; everyone wished "to better his condition"; and the majority did. But the gains were very unequally spread. A few became fabulously rich; many remained pitiably poor, and were herded in the slums of crowded cities or in the no less drab shacks of mining and factory towns. Business invaded politics, and politics became almost a synonym for corruption.

The politics of the huge city were most unblushingly without conscience; and in the nineties religion in city after city protested, and protested dramatically. In New York there was a sinister understanding between leaders in the dominant machine, which controlled the police, and those whose catering to appetites and vices required non-enforcement of law. In one of the pulpits was a scholarly New Englander, with a trenchant style, whose soul was stirred within him until on February 14, 1892, he startled a most respectable and highly educated and influential congregation by declaring:

In its municipal life our city is thoroughly rotten. Here is an immense city reaching out arms of evangelization to every quarter of the globe; and yet every step that we take looking to the moral betterment of the city has to be taken directly in the teeth of the damnable pack of administrative bloodhounds that are fattening themselves on the ethical flesh and blood of our citizenship. . . . This is not bringing politics into the pulpit. The particular political stripe of a municipal administration is no matter of our interest, and none of our business, but to strike at iniquity is part of the business of the Church, indeed it is *the* business of the Church. . . .

We have got to have a better city than this is; and men who feel iniquity keenly, and who are not afraid to stand up and hammer it unflinchingly and remorselessly, and never get tired of hammering it, are the instruments God has always used to the defeat of Satan and to the bringing in of a better day.[1]

The sermon, published in the press and widely commented on, produced a sensation. The preacher, Dr. Charles H. Parkhurst, was denounced as a traducer of the good name of the metropolis, a scandalmonger, and castigated for libeling the city's well-meaning rulers. Yet many knew that he was telling the truth, but perhaps without evidence which would stand before the courts. He and a few devoted helpers set to work to supply the deficiency.

A month later, on the morning of March 13, the place on the pulpit usually occupied by Bible and hymnbook was filled by a bulky package of affidavits. In his discourse the preacher announced:

To say that the police do not know what is going on with all the brilliant symptoms of the character of the place distinctly in view is rot. I do not ask anyone to excuse or apologize for my language. You have got to fit your words to their theme. We do not handle charcoal with a silver ladle nor carry city garbage out to the dumping ground in a steam yacht.

Dr. Parkhurst was summoned before the grand jury; he appeared with his affidavits; and the city was shaken by a moral earthquake. What took place in the metropolis was known over the country. The civic conscience developed seeing eyes and a backbone.

A religious faith which does something and keeps busily at it is congenial to the American temperament. Josiah Royce remarked that we as a people

prefer the greatness of "him that taketh a city" rather than of "him that ruleth his own spirit." [2]

One of the ministers in a midwestern city most active throughout his pastorate in its public affairs confesses:

It was not an individualistic pietism that appealed to me; it was a religion that laid hold upon life with both hands, and proposed, first and foremost, to realize the Kingdom of God in this world.[3]

Representatives of the immigrants began to capture the imagination and prick the conscience of the comfortably circumstanced by descriptions of the lot of those who had come through "the open door" to "the land of opportunity" and were in "the melting pot." The Danish newspaper reporter, Jacob Riis, with his *How the Other Half Lives,* and later the Hungarian Jew (who became a Christian minister), Edward Steiner, with his series of articles *On the Trail of the Immigrant,* and others, made the nation aware of the pitiable plight of hosts of its new inhabitants. Men saw at what human cost the prosperity of the country was piling up.

To help the underprivileged tenement-dwellers in crowded cities social settlements sprang into existence under Christian inspiration, and at the start in close association with the Church. Settlements brought educated and cultured folk to live in the midst of neighbors without their advantages, and supplied opportunities for various forms of education and recreation, as well as friendly help and counsel, and attempted to give leadership to their communities. In recent years most settlements have become entirely secular. This was due to the fact that they were for the most part Protestant while their constituencies were predominantly Roman Catholic or Jewish. Their concern has been with a larger and better life apart altogether from religious faith. The typical social worker of today lacks the religious tone and quality which characterized those of a generation ago.

About the same time Churches with similar environments began to extend their activities. They built church houses with halls for dramatic and other entertainments, with a gymnasium and rooms for classes and clubs; and they attempted to minister to the whole life, rather than only to the souls, of the population about them. Reporting on such an institutional church in 1892, its minister wrote that twelve hundred patronize the gymnasium weekly and from fifteen hundred to two thousand visit the recreation rooms:

"No need," he adds, "of talking about reaching the masses any longer. . . . We have more masses than we know what to do with. When we opened our Boys' Club, we had 570 applications in less than a week, and then we quit giving out any more for fear of a Johnstown flood of juvenile humanity." [4]

There can be no question of the social value of the work of such churches. But there have been a number of them who "reached masses" with entertainments and recreations and aided them with much-needed wholesome friendship but hardly helped form in them the mind of Christ. A congregation's work may obtain breadth at the expense of depth. No one today would wish for a less inclusive ministry to the church's neighborhood; but most spiritual leaders are resolved that the Church shall bring the thought and lives of all its adherents under the sway of Christ, making them intelligent and determined disciples with both the light and the power of the Christian Gospel.

One of the first ministers to treat the social implications of the Gospel was Dr. Washington Gladden, who preached a series of sermons and published them under the caption *Applied Christianity*. It is indicative of the novelty of the theme that the literary adviser of his Boston publishers could not see the relevance of the title.[5]

There were various ethical approaches to the question of the control and use of the new riches. In June and December, 1889, Andrew Carnegie published two articles in *The North American Review*, which at the instance of Mr. Gladstone were also printed in *The Pall Mall Gazette* under the more striking title *The Gospel of Wealth*. Mr. Carnegie laid down two postulates: first, that in the present economic system

we start with a condition of affairs under which the best interests of the race are promoted, but which inevitably gives wealth to the few;

and, second,

The millionaire will be but the trustee for the poor, intrusted for a season with a great part of the wealth of the community, but administering it for the community far better than it would or could have done for itself.[6]

Dr. William J. Tucker, then professor at Andover, replied in the *Atlantic Monthly,* stating his objection to this economic feudalism.

I can conceive of no greater mistake, more disastrous in the end to religion, if not to society, than that of trying to make charity do the work of justice.

And again:

If the few can "administer wealth" for the community "far better than it could or would do for itself," then democracy has reached the limit of its intelligence and responsibility.[7]

It was not, however, evident to numbers of Christian leaders that democratic standards could govern the world of industry. The unionization of labor was fiercely resisted, not only by employers who wished to retain autocratic control of their enterprises, but by many workers and a large section of the public who considered labor unions restrictions on the liberty of working men and women. Ministers who were convinced devotees of democracy in government accepted class distinctions as socially inevitable, and even beneficial. Dr. Henry van Dyke, speaking to future ministers, said:

Tell the Lady Bountiful that she is not called to discard her ladyhood, but to give herself with all her refinements, with all her accomplishments, with all that has been given to her of sweetness and light, to the ennobling service of humanity. Tell the Merchant-Prince that he is not called to abandon his place of influence and power, but to fill it in a princely spirit, to be a true friend and father to all who are dependent upon him, to make his prosperity a fountain of blessing to his fellow-men, to be a faithful steward of Almighty God.[8]

It was a time when capital was being put together in larger units. There was much discussion of monopolies, trusts, mergers, holding companies, "interlocking directorates," aggregated capital, "the concentrated portion of the money supply." Mr. Carnegie said of some promoters:

They throw cats and dogs together and call them elephants.[9]

John D. Rockefeller, on the contrary, believed in combinations. Attacked on the ground of the tyranny of that company in which he was conspicuous, and asked,

What did you do with those who refused to come in with you?

he replied:

We left them to the mercy of time; they could not hope to compete with us.[10]

A book which had a wide circulation in the early nineties bore the title *Wealth against Commonwealth*.[11] Religious leaders, who for the most part accepted the current economic order although they wished its faults amended, began to scrutinize it much more critically. A few advocated its more socialistic reorganization.

One of these, who published a number of books and had a considerable following among students, Dr. George D. Herron, taught a merging of Christianity and politics.

The civilization of today is a camp of a vast unorganized and undisciplined army, without visible or apparent method, yet consciously preparing for some nearing conflict which shall issue in a new beginning of history. . . . Society is moving quickly toward revolution; but it is revolution from anarchy to order, from industrial slavery to industrial freedom, from social violence to social peace, from political atheism to the kingdom of God.[12]

He then stated a new Christian apocalyptic:

The political appearing of Christ is manifest in the increasing social functions of the state.[13]

Looking at Europe and our own country forty-five years later, how naive seems this faith that the augmentation of the social functions of government can of itself be identified with a divine advent!

The demonic forces of that decade seemed to him the railways. By the nineties in the minds of reformers they had taken the place occupied in a previous generation by slavery. They were the debasers of legislatures and courts.

The year following the publication of this book of Professor Herron's saw the country plunged in a political campaign when the social issue was brought to the fore, although in a somewhat crude form, by the championship of the rights of the agriculturists and manual workers as against the financiers. William Jennings Bryan won the nomination for President in the Democratic Convention by a dramatic speech which declaimed:

You shall not press down upon the brow of labor this crown of thorns, you shall not crucify mankind upon a cross of gold.[14]

Men like Professor Herron (to return to him) helped to make sensitive the Christian social conscience. He pled:

The regenerated individual must bear, and ought to bear, the humiliation and perplexity, the social guilt and retribution, of the sins of the system in which he lives; . . . his food and clothing, his money and his bread, the home in which he lives and the books he reads, the school in which he learns and the pulpit under which he worships, are all stained with the blood of the social victims.[15]

And while he believed in human effort, he was not guilty of the current assurance in man's power:

Our national salvation will not come from our own baffled thought, or be the gain of our confused and ignorant efforts, but will come as the gift of God, who shall ordain peace for us when His Spirit shall have wrought in us His salvation and social justice. . . . The faith that God through Christ will save society will not paralyze our reform activities, nor shake our readiness to be offered in behalf of our brothers, but will divinely energize us to the most strenuous activity.[16]

It was an evidence of the deeper probing of Christian thinkers into the causes of social ills when in 1905 there arose a controversy over the action of the leaders of a foreign mission board in soliciting a gift from Mr. Rockefeller, Sr. Dr. Gladden led an attack against accepting "partnership with plunderers," and the pulpits discussed "tainted money." The result, however, was a drawn battle.

Shortly thereafter an indictment of the whole social order from a Christian standpoint was made by Dr. Walter Rauschenbusch in a book which was read by most ministers and many laymen, *Christianity and the Social Crisis:*

The essential purpose of Christianity (is) to transform human society into the kingdom of God by regenerating all human relations and reconstituting them in accordance with the will of God.[17]

The Church has often rendered valuable aid in its protest against some single intolerable evil, but it has accepted as inevitable the general social system under which the world was living at the time, and has not undertaken any thoroughgoing social reconstruction in accordance with Christian principles.[18]

In a later book he amplified this denunciation of the Church's circumscription of its task:

To become fully Christian the Church must come out of its spiritual isolation. In theory and practice the Church has long constituted a world by itself. It has been governed by ecclesiastical motives and interests which are often remote from the real interests of humanity, and has almost uniformly set Church questions ahead of social questions. It has often built a soundproof habitation in which people could live for years without becoming definitely conscious of the existence of prostitution, child labor, and tenement crowding. It has offered peace and spiritual tranquillity to men and women who needed thunderclaps and lightnings. Like all the rest of us, the Church will get salvation by finding the purpose of its existence outside of itself, in the kingdom of God, the perfect life of the race.[19]

Some of the leaders in the social application of Christianity became avowed socialists in politics and a former Christian minister became the outstanding candidate of that party in election after election. But political socialism won a very small following.

Today it is recognized that many of the ministers interested in the social application of Christianity went too far in the discussion of politics and economics in the pulpit. Norman Thomas, the socialist candidate to whom I have referred, has said:

A preacher has a right and a duty to be a citizen and to take part with other citizens in political and social life. He has neither the right nor the duty to turn the Christian pulpit into a lecture platform from which he pontificates on social subjects in which he has no particular training and no imperative message. The man who wants to discuss current events from a genuine liberal point of view makes a great mistake if he thinks that desire is a call to the ministry. The Church may well, as one of its activities, promote discussion of current problems, but no church justifies itself simply by becoming a forum. Indeed, I should go further. I do not think that the Church, at any rate the Christian Church, has any particular significance for society except as it has something fundamental to say about the universe and man's relation to it. That is to say about metaphysics, or more concretely, theology. For the minister a social conscience and some humanitarian enthusiasm are no substitutes for a living message about a God in whose love and power he has found not only his own peace but also his ground for hope for the victory of the Kingdom of God and the peace of all mankind.[20]

The major achievement of preachers of the Christian social ethic was the creation of a new mind on economic issues. In 1915, writing in the *Atlantic Monthly,* President Tucker summed up the change:

The social conscience has done very much to refurnish the public mind with ideas and principles and with conceptions of duty fit and adequate to the new demands of society. In particular it may be claimed that it has reinstated the conception of justice above that of charity in the ethics of philanthropy; that it has recalled liberty to a service in behalf of political freedom; that it has awakened "a sense of the state" corresponding to the increase of political responsibilities; that it has made society sensitive to the inhumanities of industrialism, and is teaching society to estimate the property rights which are involved in human rights; and that it is creating an open mind toward the entrance of woman into civic life.[21]

But in connection with woman and the home it must be granted that the social development of the last fifty years shows mixed results. The equality of the sexes is generally recognized; but divorce has increased threefold in proportion to the number of marriages. The causes for the increase are various —woman's economic independence, an exaggerated individualism in both men and women placing personal happiness before social obligation, the relative ease and cheapness with which freedom from marital ties can be obtained, the change in public sentiment toward divorce, *et cetera*. But children of broken homes rarely escape serious harm. Few Protestant Christians advocate abolition of divorce, but most desire uniform laws throughout the land and more Christian education concerning marriage. The social conscience has hardly shown an advance during the half century in this basic human relationship.

The sharpening of Christian consciences with regard to other social injustices had significant religious results. Throughout Yesterday one heard lamentations among Church folk over the disappearance of the sense of sin. The evangelists of the sixties and seventies spoke to persons troubled with guilt for their misdoings and aware of man's lost estate. Evolutionary science and philosophical immanentism altered the popular mood. Men wished to become their true selves; and if they felt hindered, they ascribed their frustration to their animal inheritance or their faulty environment. They were not abased before God with a feeling of personal sinfulness. Gradually in the late nineties and the early years of this century, sin was extended to include corporate iniquities. Men became aware of their implication in social neglects and unrighteousness.

A small book by a sociologist, who had lost his position in Stanford University by his outspoken condemnation of the ruthless, and often lawless, acts of powerful corporations, was introduced to the public with a letter from President Theodore Roosevelt. Its title was *Sin and Society,* and in it Professor Edward A. Ross coined the phrase "sinning by syndicate." Amplifying this expression, he wrote:

Take the face-to-face element out of a relation, and any lurking devil in it comes to the surface. . . . There is nothing like distance to disinfect dividends. Therefore the moral character of the stockholders makes very little difference in the conduct of the affairs of the corporation. . . . The business man may be swerved by vindictiveness or by generosity, by passion or by conscience, but the genuine corporation responds to but one motive. Toward gain it gravitates with the ruthlessness of a lava stream.

You can hiss the bad man, lampoon him, caricature him, ostracize him and his. Not so with the bad corporation. The corporation is not in dread of hell fire. You cannot Christianize it. You may convert its stockholders, animate them with patriotism or public spirit or love of social service; but this will have little or no effect on the tenor of their corporation. . . . Public indignation meets a cuirass of divided responsibility that scatters a shock which would have stretched iniquity prone.[22]

Such preaching from the printed page and from many a platform as well as from the pulpit gave the conscientious a new sense of their involvement in the evils of society. This extension and deepening of the consciousness of sin has continued to grow. Who was chargeable with the World War? who caused a miscarriage of ideals in the Peace of Versailles? who is to blame for the economic ills and the mad outbreaks of repressed peoples? Such questions have probed the consciences of men and made them see guilty footprints at their own doors. Instead of the light-hearted optimism of Yesterday, the present generation is burdened with the world's wrongs and woes, for which our country. our economic order, our race are in part responsible, and every individual shares in the corporate guilt.

The Christian Gospel in its typical expositions among the preachers of Yesterday laid little stress upon the cross. The principal doctrine of the earlier evangelicism had been the Atonement. Christians had felt a boundless devotion to a Saviour who had borne their sins at Calvary and made possible their salvation. The hymnals of the seventies and eighties, and especially the Gospel Hymns, show this as the central theme of praise.

> I will sing the wondrous story
> Of the Christ who died for me,
> How He left His home in glory
> For the Cross on Calvary.[23]

But two or three decades later such ideas had little force with any but traditionalists. In their sturdy individualism men asked, How could one bear the sin of another? In any case was not "sin" an outworn word which psychologists were showing up as the delusion of an unhealthy mind? At most was it not a label for an impotence to be got rid of or for a past slip to be forgotten? But when sin is viewed in its social context, the cross of Christ becomes the supreme instance of the tragic consequences well-meaning individuals bring about in their corporate relations. Jesus is the victim of ecclesiasticism, economic privilege, political expediency, mob hysteria, militarism, public apathy. His very crucifixion—a horribly degrading form of public execution from which Roman citizens were exempt, reserved for contemptible provincials—is an evidence of social discrimination. At the cross one sees the solidarity of evil combining its forces to do away with the Son of God. The factors which dominate our world are exposed in their hideous form as nowhere else.

Jesus' voluntary submission to death is the supreme disclosure of a social conscience—a conscience to which the sins of His nation, His Church, His world are His own. And dying, the Righteous for the unrighteous, He becomes the Creator of a new community, whose life is His Spirit of love. To its members He in His cross is the revelation of His Father's forgiveness, who bears His children's sin on His heart and is ever giving Himself to redeem them.

The social interpretation of Christianity led to an emphasis upon other aspects of God. Some theologians insisted upon the social nature of God Himself. Dr. George A. Gordon, for example, using the Trinitarian formula, wrote:

Put into the Godhead some reality answering to the words the Father and the Son and the Holy Spirit, and one is able to conceive of God's existence as ineffably blessed, and as containing in itself the ground of human society.[24]

President McGiffert, who was not attracted to this "divine commonwealth," said:

The social emphasis rather suggests the socializing of

Deity by recognizing God's connection with men, or better the enlarging of humanity by extending the boundaries of society to include God as well as men.[25]

The New Testament expression "the kingdom of God" was seized on and made to stand for the consummation of current social hopes. The words originally meant "the reign of God," and the emphasis had been upon His accomplishment of its triumph. But with the current emphasis upon man's activity in religion, he was frequently spoken of as the builder of the kingdom. Indeed the word "kingdom" was unpalatable to ardent devotees of democracy, and they substituted for it "the commonwealth of God." Some went so far as to speak of a "democratic God." Dr. George A. Coe wrote:

Religion becomes so ultra-radical as to raise the question whether there is justice in the cosmic order itself, and to undertake social enterprises of cosmic scope, such as the promotion of the universal democracy of God.[26]

If this phrase means more than that the Lord of the universe is the companionable Father of the children of men, it is absurd. Democracy is an irrelevant word in connection with One whom men do not elect to His rulership and whom they cannot retire.

He sits on no precarious throne,
Nor borrows leave to be.

If God be love, as Christ revealed, His nature is inherently social.

It was upon this more conscientious and socially-minded America and world that the Great War broke as a horrifying surprise. By a large section of church-going people war had come to be regarded as a moral impossibility. Scientific discoveries and inventions had rendered it too destructive and terrible to contemplate. Humanitarianism had made such strides among civilized men that it was unthinkable that they should engage in mass slaughter. The network of modern commerce and finance had bound the nations in so close an economic unity that business leaders would not consent to its rupture. Labor had attained an international solidarity, and the workers would refuse to be led against one another. War was *The Great Illusion*.[27] The Church must create a spiritual fellowship which would bind mankind in one. This had been stressed at international missionary assemblies, notably that held in Edinburgh in 1910. The following year a delegation of German Church leaders had made a journey to Britain to form the "Associated Council of the Churches of the British and German Empires for fostering friendly relations." In welcoming them the London *Times* reports the Archbishop of Canterbury as saying:

They wanted each of the two great nations to have at its centre a solid corps of men and women thus vivified (by the power of the Holy Spirit, and the spirit of Christian brotherhood), and they believed that in that way they would bring about what would make the bare possibility of war, or the spirit and tone which gave rise to war, first unlikely, then difficult, ultimately quite impossible.

And it reports Professor Adolf Harnack as replying:

We dare not cast forth this ideal (of human brotherhood proclaimed by Christ) from the realm of politics; we are bound to recognize its validity even there. We ought not to act as if our Christianity bound us only in the home and in the Church, whilst elsewhere its authority failed; as if the sword of the barbarian maintained a lawful place among us.[28]

At this side of the Atlantic churchmen took an active part in opposing any increase in the navy, and computed what the cost of a single battleship might do in education or slum clearance. The country was overwhelmingly pacifist.

The ineptitudes and ruthlessness of the Germans, skillful propaganda on the part of the Allies, the

underlying kinship of Anglo-Saxon ideals, and finally the statement of our purposes in entering into the
conflict as they were phrased by a notable Christian
president satisfied the consciences and aroused the
devotion of the vast majority of American Christians.
Phrases like "the war to end war," or "to make the
world safe for democracy," or to give enslaved peoples the right of self-determination, appealed to deep-
seated moral instincts. Whatever may be said now
of the irresistible pressure of financial interests, of
these the American public was not then aware.[29] It
was embarking upon another crusade. Hundreds
of thousands, both younger and older, shared the
feelings which T. E. Lawrence tells us possessed him:

It felt like morning, and the freshness of the world-to-
be intoxicated us. We were wrought up with ideals
inexpressible and vaporous, but to be fought for.[30]

When the War was done, and the Peace of Versailles published, and the disillusionizing years rolled
over us, Lawrence's further words, after his experiences with politicians who destroyed one by one
the commitments he had made with his Arab associates, could also phrase the feelings of millions
among ourselves:

When we achieved and the new world dawned, the old

141

men came out again and took from us our victory, and re-made it in the likeness of the former world they knew. Youth could win, but had not learned to keep, and was pitiably weak against age. We stammered that we had worked for a new heaven and a new earth, and they thanked us kindly and made their peace.[30]

The disillusionment did not come as swiftly here as abroad. The prosperity which prevailed in the twenties kept the nation hopeful, and its social idealism continued strong. Some churchmen hailed the Russian experiment as a signal illustration of the embodiment of Christian principles,[31] even when Christian convictions were fiercely denounced and the Church cruelly persecuted. But the purges by the dominant group after a time alienated most Christian sympathizers, and today Russian Communism is as unblushingly imperialistic as Capitalism at its worst. The sharp challenge which the totalitarian states have thrown down to ideals American Christians have taken for granted—international co-operation, humanitarianism, democracy in government, personal liberty, the rights of minorities, tolerance, the spiritual independence of the Church —have produced a new state of mind.

We see a revolt against Liberalism. The Nineteenth Century had no more heartily cherished word among the peoples of Western Europe and America.

Like all noble words—the word "Christian" among the rest—it was used very loosely, often to cover everything which a speaker considered desirable. It was widely identified with faith in man, in his science, in his inevitable progress, in the power of reason to solve all problems. Today this faith is questioned or denied. But Liberalism is fundamentally an attitude toward truth. It involves faith in man's capacity to discern truth when it is presented to him. In its essence it is a resolve to welcome truth even when most unpleasant and to be obedient to it. It is an attitude which goes back at least to ancient Greece, and has its counterpart in the pursuit of wisdom by the Hebrew sages. It has, therefore, a religious origin—loyalty to truth because truth is an aspect of God. A liberal today is not less a liberal if he does not share the boundless confidence in man, or in his science, or in his inevitable progress, or in the power of reason to solve all problems. If he does not believe that these are true, as a liberal he must reject them. None the less he continues to face facts, to strive for freedom to investigate all things and freedom to teach and speak what one believes to be true. There can be no education worthy the name, and no science or art or vital religion, without this freedom.

The twenties, which felt the reaction from the

idealism of the War, were a lean decade for religion. It seemed in retreat on college campuses; missions were less generously sustained in the Churches; Christian convictions, and especially Christian ethics, were ridiculed by intellectuals. A typical book was Walter Lippmann's *A Preface to Morals,* which scorned the faith of all Churches and substituted a disinterested devotion to social well-being based on a scientific outlook upon the world. But today, with totalitarian nations rampant, Mr. Lippmann is again representative of many when he writes:

> Collectivist regimes are always profoundly irreligious. For religious experience entails the recognition of an inviolable essence in men; it cultivates a self-respect and a self-reliance, which tend at some point to resist the total subjection of the individual to any earthly power. By the religious experience the humblest communicant is led into the presence of a power so much greater than his master's that the distinctions of this world are of little importance. So it is no accident that the only open challenge to the totalitarian state has come from men of deep religious faith. For in their faith they are vindicated as immortal souls, and from this enhancement of their dignity they find the reason why they must offer a perpetual challenge to the dominion of men over men.[32]

Generally among the thoughtful there is a feeling that the solution of our world's ills must be spiritual, and there is a hospitality and wistfulness for a religion which can bind nations and races in fellowship and enlarge the soul of man to match and master his augmented physical powers.

In this country and Britain there is a new recognition of the necessity of a spiritual foundation for democracy. The democratic way of life and of government was born chiefly of the Hebrew-Christian tradition; it did not spring up in any other quarter of the earth but that in which Christian ideas were assumed. It rests on a threefold faith—faith in the capacities of the common man, faith in the self-evidencing power of truth and righteousness, faith in a just Lord of the universe who has so fashioned and orders it that men and nations can live together satisfactorily only in brotherhood. It is noteworthy that at the moment there is among educators and thoughtful people generally a dissatisfaction with our secular system of education. Without the religious convictions concerning God and man, of which democracy sprang, it is robbed of its vitalizing ideology, and is likely to perish. The decisive battlefield on which it will win or be lost is in minds and consciences. No education for democracy can afford to neglect its spiritual bases. Its best propaganda is the publicizing throughout the world of the central beliefs of the Gospel, and their social incarnation in commonwealths which seriously attempt to give all their people justice and liberty.

The consecration of religious people to a more just society remains, although the more pessimistic outlook of our time sees the kingdom of God lying beyond human history and to be achieved by Him. It rightly insists that any social order of man's devising will bear the marks of his ignorance and sin; it cannot be the kingdom of God. But this reaction goes too far. While we cannot identify any visions of ours, however lofty, with the final purpose of God, we believe that our Christian hopes are prompted by His Spirit. The forms in which we clothe them—in economics and politics, in domestic and international relations—are ours, and marred by our limitations and evil. But God has made known His eternal purpose in Christ, and to seek to be ruled by that purpose and to strive for its embodiment in every sphere of life is surely preparing for God's reign. Its complete realization lies beyond history; but history should be the record of a race under education for fellowship with God and with one another in Him. He who is the Light of the eternal city is also the Light of the world.

Chapter VI

THE CHURCH

In addition to the movements in religion Yesterday which were affected by factors in contemporary thought, the life of the Church in this country developed in response to changing needs in the social scene and under the inspiration of various forces, some from within and some from without the Church's own fellowship.

There was a special concern for children and young people. This was in part due to the growing urbanization of life with the weakening of home education, and in part to the necessity of reaching the numbers of children of the immigrants. Sunday schools reached their peak in attendance in Yesterday. Most of them had a single lesson which teachers adapted to the ages of the pupils in their classes, and oldest and youngest studied the same passage of Scripture, and memorized the same Golden Text. The whole school assembled for an opening and a closing service, in which stress was laid on hearty singing. In cities there were large schools, occasionally presided over by celebrities, like the Hon. John Wanamaker in Philadelphia—an outstanding merchant and a member of the Cabinet, but no less faithful and hard-working in his leadership of his Sunday school. Adult Bible classes also sought prominent men or women as teachers and some of them built up a wide following. The physical arrangements for such schools brought a new form of architecture, with numerous small classrooms opening off a central auditorium. Sliding doors and movable partitions made it possible to throw the whole building into one large assembly hall. In such schools education was largely exhortation. Every teacher and the superintendent were preachers.

The uniform lesson for all ages fell under the condemnation of educators, who pointed out that the Biblical material was not equally fitted to all, and should not be offered to pupils for whom it was irrelevant or inappropriate. This led to the preparation and wide use of graded lessons. There was a theory, sponsored by Dr. G. Stanley Hall, that a child recapitulates the spiritual evolution of the race.[1] The more primitive parts of the Bible should, therefore, be given to younger children, and the Christian Gospel with its altruistic ethic reserved for their later years. There is something in this theory, but happily in practice it was never rigidly adhered to. Young children were not taught to be animists and, later, adherents of a tribal Jehovah; but the Lord's Prayer and New Testament verses were committed to memory in the youngest class, and in hymns Christ was adored as Master and Friend.

This was the epoch when young people's societies attained their maximum popularity. The United Society of Christian Endeavor, founded by Francis E. Clark in 1885, attempted to enlist the young people of all the Protestant communions in one organization, and to train them in active participation in worship, in evangelism, in various forms of service for the community, and to stimulate their loyalty to the Church and increase their efficiency in its work. Its unifying aim was not altogether successful, for denominationalism was still strong, and several communions established similar societies of their own. But for more than a decade it held huge annual conventions which promoted mass enthusiasm; and some later Church mergers, notably that which produced the United Church of Canada, are partially to be ascribed to the leadership of those who as younger folk were trained by it.

On the campuses of the colleges and universities there were vigorous student Christian associations, which were centers of Bible study, of evangelism, and of recruiting for the ministry, the mission field, and the leadership of the Church. They, too, had annual conferences, of which those at Northfield, Massachusetts, under the personal guidance of Dwight L. Moody, became the type. In them by the hundreds students were faced with the Christian message, with the spiritual needs of the world, and with the responsibility which God had placed on them. Most of the Christian leaders of the next generation owed an incalculable debt to this movement, and it is significant that the outstanding figures in the Ecumenical Movement of our time are in large part its products. Dr. John R. Mott is a typical example.

The desire to enlist in their service the host of eager young people led to modifications in the life and work of the Churches. Church buildings were added to or made over to provide meeting rooms, and sometimes facilities for recreation. Services of public worship became more informal and friendly. Instead of the staid and reverent gathering of an earlier day, the assembly of an American congregation had a lively tone. The architecture of churches underwent a change in the latter years of the Nineteenth Century. Aesthetically the change was for the worse, for the taste of the period was poor. But the change was due partly to practical reasons—the provision for the Sunday school and the young people's meetings, and partly to the prevailing ideal of worship. Instead of the assembly of devout folk to offer their homage to the Lord of earth and heaven and to hear His sovereign will in His revealed Word, it was a gathering of the household of the heavenly Father, whose chief desire was that they edify one another and bring home His indifferent and erring children. Churches were built with an eye to comfort and sociability; they were not designed to foster adoration. Pews were frequently placed in circles which sloped like an amphitheater, so that every seat commanded an uninterrupted view of pulpit and choir. The minister was placed on a platform, instead of in the high pulpit of the colonial epoch. The choir was usually behind him and facing the congregation so as to be heard most effectively. A capacious vestibule supplied a place where strangers could be welcomed and the entering and departing congregation could chat. The end of the edifice toward which the congregation looked was often filled with the gilded pipes of an organ, as though noise were the chief matter to be symbolized. There were few or no symbols from the Christian tradition, although the open Bible on the pulpit and the Communion Table had their momentous import. The immanent Father was within the hearts of His children met to express and augment their faith and

151

hope and love, and the assembly was itself the chief symbol of the indwelling God.

It is noteworthy that more recently constructed churches are built on other lines. Many of them are Gothic and seem somewhat unrelated to the type of worship carried on in them. Many of them appear more imitative of admired buildings of the past than designed with a view to the functions they fulfill in today. This is peculiarly the case where the niches and stained-glass windows are filled with figures of saints whose names are unknown to American Christians. Others attempt to reproduce the older churches of our colonial period. The significant point is that the newer types of building restore the conception of worship as God-centered—the offering of adoration, penitence, and prayer to Him. Reverence is again taking the place of sociability. God is not to be seen mainly in man, even in fellow Christians; He remains above the saintliest, other and loftier than man at his best. These more recent edifices are usually more austere in color and line than were those of the nineties; no less attention has been paid to comfort, but an effort has been made not to hold attention to things visible, but to give the mind incentive to focus upon the Unseen. It is evident that Christians wish again the house of God, rather than the meeting place of His friendly people.

The music of the Church had undergone a change which became generally accepted in the hymnals of our Yesterday. The secular part-song had been taken by British composers and used as the model of hymn tunes with elaborate harmonizations which demanded a more rapid rendering than the older psalm tunes. Outstanding among these composers who revolutionized the taste of congregations at both sides of the Atlantic were the Rev. John B. Dykes, Sir Joseph Barnby, Sir Arthur Sullivan (even better known for his operettas written in collaboration with Sir W. S. Gilbert), W. H. Monk, the musical editor of *Hymns Ancient and Modern,* and Sir John Stainer. They and their imitators awoke an instantaneous response in the devout of that day. A New England professor, writing to an editor of one of the hymnals, said:

Those other tunes—of Monk and Dykes and Stainer and Barnby and Tours *et al*—just lift one's soul up into heaven. . . . I hope those composers will go into the heavenly life with their creative powers all perfect and forever increasing.[2]

Along with these more formal tunes Gospel Hymns were in wide use. To the taste of Today both the choir music and the favorite hymn tunes of that epoch seem sentimental.

Shortly after the turn of the Century a reaction began in Britain and has been increasingly felt in this country since about 1910. It has not led to the composition of a great number of new tunes; but rather to the restoration of earlier Church music: Plain song, Chorales, the tunes of the Genevan and other psalters, carols and other folk melodies. There has been a revival of Bach and of earlier Italian composers of Church music. University choirs are singing almost none of the anthems which were heard in chapels in the nineties. A new standard of music has been set which at once satisfies aesthetic judgment and seems congruous with the more august conception of Deity to whom our age looks in adoration.[3]

The quartet was a popular form of choir in our Yesterday. It fitted the tune which emphasized its harmonies. But quartets led congregational singing ineffectively: if the quartet was good, the people listened to it; if it was poor, it lacked power to lead. The "song leader," with whom young people had become familiar at conferences, was introduced into services of public worship, and often brought with him the informal methods and manners of the conference, calling on the men in the congregation to sing one verse, the women another, persons in the galleries a third, or himself rendering a verse and asking the congregation to join in the chorus. Such usages fostered heartiness and general participation, but concentrated attention on the singing rather than on God to whom the praise was offered.

In the nineties psychologists began to turn their investigations upon worship.[4] It was inevitable that they should assess it for its effects upon those who participated in it. They helped to banish hymns with unwholesome suggestions, to frown on the introspective piety quite widely cultivated, to check emotionalism, and to bring worship to the test of its social consequences. But their work tended to make worship even more man-regarding. It was not an offering to God for His purposes; it was a means of producing religious experiences in worshipers. Protestants generally ceased to consider their attendance at public worship as corporate homage to God; it was an exercise in which they engaged for the development of their own characters and those of fellow worshipers. Hence if they did not feel it to be interesting or inspiring, they stayed away, and sought other stimulation of their devout emotions. Emily Dickinson, whose poems first saw publication in the nineties, is typical of this revolt from the obligation of corporate worship:

> Some keep the Sabbath going to church;
> I keep it staying at home,

With a bobolink for a chorister,
And an orchard for a dome.

Some keep the Sabbath in surplice;
I just wear my wings,
And instead of tolling the bell for church,
Our little sexton sings.

God preaches—a noted clergyman—
And the sermon is never long;
So instead of getting to heaven at last,
I'm going all along.

Her lines evidence the extreme individualism of the current religion, and her preoccupation with the effect of worship on her own feelings: self-satisfaction on the self's loftiest level was the aim. She is oblivious of the historic Christian conception of worship as the Church's sacrifice of praise and prayer and of the consecration to God of the Body of Christ in sermon and sacrament. This is a conception which our day is recovering.

But Emily Dickinson spoke of "keeping the Sabbath." With the change in our population due to the incoming of millions without the Anglo-Saxon tradition, and with the rapid growth of Sunday sports and entertainments and the coming of the automobile opening up long ranges of travel and visiting, the American Sunday became less and less a Sabbath. One of our contemporaries, looking back on the Sunday still usual in the nineties, writes: "The rhythm of the day was different."

The mind, freed from weekly routine, and held back from active pleasure, did quietly fit meditation to the Sunday rhythm and mingle with boredom a sedate happiness, which is one of the experiences that I believe is now lost.[5]

A periodic sedative, tranquilizing the minds of the American public, is patently desirable. A change in the rhythm of our overactive lives would have beneficent effect on nerves and characters. If this change in rhythm for one day a week led to meditation, and particularly to meditation upon God and life in harmony with Him, it would be spiritually enriching. But there is as yet no sign of a restoration of the Sabbath.

We have spoken of the emphasis in Yesterday upon the Fatherhood of God. Devout folk felt confident that in this they were returning to the religion of Jesus Himself. But a change had begun to occur in the relations of parents and children of which they were only partially aware. The Victorian parent believed that he possessed authority over his sons and daughters and expected deference from them. "Honor thy father and thy mother" was a commandment still in force. But in the nineties, and more generally in the first decades of this century, fathers and mothers were trying hard to be "good pals" with their children. "Father and Son" dinners or athletic contests, sponsored by Young Men's Christian Associations and similar agencies, idealized this new comradeship. Among the millions of immigrants flocking into our ports it was the children who first acquired our language and learned the ways of their new environment. With free education in school and college open to them, they swiftly became the economic superiors of their parents, finding more remunerative employment and rising to a new social level. This tended to reverse normal relations between the generations. Sons and daughters became the guides of their parents into the novel life of their adopted country and the arbiters of the home. Traditional respect for age was swept away. Indeed after the Great War it was common to blame the older generation for wrecking mankind, and youth was repeatedly told, and often told itself, that it alone had the capacity to build a brave new world. An absurd self-assurance was fostered in the young. This was evident in the nineteen-twenties. The generations not only met on terms of equality, but elders humbled themselves before the young.

This had a subtle effect on religion. Devout

158

American Christians, teaching their children that
God was a father, and thinking that they were im-
parting the faith of Jesus, lost sight of the vast difference between an American father and the Jewish
father of the time of Christ. The elements of authority and awe, stressed in the Palestinian home,
had gone from the parental relation. There was a
tone of familiarity in men's attitudes toward the
Most High. The devout had been spoken of as
"God-fearing"; but that designation no longer fitted
the devout of our Yesterday. Men, like Abraham
Lincoln, had referred to God as their Maker. Under
the influence of evolutionary science that expression
dropped out of usage, and with it went the sense
of creatureliness and utter dependence upon God.
The emphasis upon human dignity raised man to a
height where he viewed the Almighty as an equal.

They stand up when He passes by, gentlemen un-
afraid.

Were men not being taught that they were co-
creators with the Lord of the universe? Indeed had
not the Lord somewhat bungled the construction of
the world, and was He not urgently needing men to
repair, improve, and complete His handiwork?

Some religious leaders in the nineties sensed the
danger in the current conception of the relations

of the Father in heaven and His human sons and daughters. Dr. Parkhurst insisted that "God is a father, not a grandfather." While the status of American parents has not changed, our present awareness of human sinfulness and frailty and the stress upon the superhumanity of God are in the way of restoring us to a more Christian religion. There is peril that the preaching of the "otherness" of God may obscure that kinship between God and man which made possible His revelation of Himself to us, and above all which enabled Him to become incarnate in the Man of Nazareth. "Father" must remain the chief name for the Divine. Professor Ralph Barton Perry writes:

The Father who pities His children is the superlatively appropriate symbol of God, not because the worshiper, being one of the children, may hope to profit by paternal indulgence, but because all-reaching and infinitely patient love is the one thing supremely worshipful.[6]

And in his last book Dr. George A. Gordon, who never minimized the august character of the Most High Sovereign of all worlds nor forgot the infinite mystery which surrounds Him, said:

A parent is the responsible author of the life of another and therefore under the most sacred obligation to care for that life. We apply this to God. . . . I confess that I stand nowhere more at peace than I do on this ground. When I implicate the honor of God and involve His whole character with the tragedy of time, I am sure that I am rendering Him the homage of the absolute truth; I thus declare my belief that He will stand by His infinite obligation to His rational creatures in this world. If that is not homage, I do not know the meaning of the word.[7]

Still another change in a human relationship—that of teacher and student—took place in our Yesterday. The Victorian schoolmaster and college professor had regarded himself as charged with the responsibility of transmitting the heritage of learning, awaking minds to think and appreciate, and molding the characters of his pupils. But in the nineties instructors began to say that they were fellow-seekers after truth and companions with their students in the quest for knowledge. By the first decade of the new century progressive educators were banning authoritarian teaching as an educational crime. The discussion group became a lauded technique. The elective system, introduced and made popular by President Charles W. Eliot, shifted the planning of his curriculum from the faculty to the student himself. His mind was to be disciplined, not by studying what maturer judgments considered wise for him to know, but by his free choice of subjects and courses, with all the risks of loss and waste involved in an unwise choice. Some went so far as to say that it made no difference what a student studied so long as he studied it scientifically. It was not the content of the curriculum but the technique of investigation that mattered. Teachers shrank from molding characters; it was their task to stimulate the young to self-realization. Ultraprogressive education went to ridiculous lengths in encouraging self-expression without attempting to furnish the self with anything valuable to express. From a Christian standpoint the sinfulness of man, young and old—his egoism and pride—was forgotten. So was the sinfulness of human society; and education which aided the young to express themselves and adjust to their communities often augmented tendencies contrary to the Christian standard.

This revolt against authoritarianism in education showed itself in a corresponding change among certain religious leaders. Authority had attached to the intellectual content of revelation—"what man is to believe concerning God and what duty God requires of man." Now it became the compulsion of the Divine fellowship. Dr. McGiffert describes the trend as follows:

Revelation is the awakening of the human consciousness to the presence of the divine, or the eliciting of
human devotion to a divine ideal; and to be religious is simply to have this consciousness or this
devotion. But where religion and revelation are thus
interpreted, authority is a matter of small moment.
It is not authority we need, but inspiration; not a code
or rule or creed or system of doctrines, but the presence
of God and the compulsion of a divine purpose. Codes
and rules are mechanical and cramping in their effects.
Spiritual and ethical maturity is attained only when dependence upon them is outgrown. It is not simply that
this idea of religious authority has changed, but that
the need of it has ceased. We are living in an age when
communion in religious things and co-operation in all
good works are becoming more and more generally possible to those whose religious beliefs, like their philosophical and scientific beliefs, are widely diverse; when not
creed but purpose is the force that binds men together
in a common institution and a common cause.[8]

Dr. Coe went even farther when he wrote:

The authority of religion is not the compulsion of a
theory, but the impulsion of our whole higher self.
Authority in religion cannot be escaped. It is not an
invention, it is not a product of thought, it is not a
tradition—it is a law of life. . . . It is within us. It is
what we are demanding to express itself, to be fed, to
grow. It is as natural and inevitable as our instincts,
and what we call submission to it is nothing but self-
expression in one of its highest forms.[9]

163

Today we find ourselves in a world where Christianity is opposed by hostile ideologies. Fascism and Communism have convictions (perhaps we should say *had* convictions at their outset). It is the definiteness of their doctrines which accounts for much of their power as religions. They have views of the world and consequent principles of action. Dr. McGiffert may be correct in saying that spiritual maturity outgrows codes and creeds, but does man attain spiritual maturity in this world? Is there any spiritual Adult save God and that Son in whom His fullness dwelleth? While revelation is the disclosure of the presence of God, God so revealed in fellowship with man has a distinctive and specific character. He is Christlike love. The intellectual content of revelation cannot be minimized. We may not be able to phrase it in precise definitions, but we know what manner of Being He is with whom we have to do, for we see Him in the face of Jesus Christ; and we also know what manner of men we must be when, confronted with the Lord on the New Testament pages, we hear His "Follow Me." Nor is this revelation of God "what we are demanding to express itself." It is what we are not, condemning what we are, making us cry out for His deliverance and offering us Himself to re-create us in His likeness.

164

Bolder spirits in a relatively recent Yesterday declared the title "Lord" obsolete. It affronted their democratic ears. It confined ethically advancing humanity within the "Jesus-stereotype" of the First Century. It stunted independence and repressed originality. Some would allow Jesus the title of "Leader," but balked at calling Him "Lord." [10] But today we confront totalitarian systems, claiming the unquestioning and whole-souled allegiance of those upon whom they are imposed. It is this completeness and exclusiveness of their demands which makes them rival religions. The religion of the Bible makes no less exigent claims upon men. "Thou shalt love the Lord thy God with all thy heart, and with all thy mind, and with all thy strength." The devotee of the Christ in the New Testament asks but one question: "Lord, what wilt Thou have me to do?" Nor are the convictions of those who yield themselves and their all to the claims of God in Christ less clear and cogent than the convictions of the most fanatical adherents of current rival faiths. We are not asked to yield unquestioning obedience. We are to bring our critical faculties as well as our hearts and consciences to the service of our Lord, and use them freely. He seeks not blind, but open-eyed obedience. He is light, and in His light we see, and can take our course and address our tasks not as slaves, but as friends of His and sons of God. Nor is originality discouraged; on the contrary He who is making all things new releases surprising powers in His faithful followers, enabling them to surprise their generation. Under Christ's lordship they become creative free men.

Nor does it seem as likely to us, as it did to Dr. Mc-Giffert three decades ago, that "co-operation in all good works" is "generally possible to those whose religious beliefs are widely diverse." At Oxford in July, 1937, the Ecumenical Conference on Life and Work discovered that differences in practical plans root in differences in theological belief. Any reader of its literature will find as much doctrinal discussion as in the subsequent conference on Faith and Order. It is still true that every act has a thought for its ancestor and there can be no united program for the Christian Church without an underlying ecumenical theology—basic convictions which hold the minds of all church folk in accord. This doctrinal agreement will never be complete, nor should it be expected in detail, but without a common Christian faith it is futile to expect united action in a common Christian purpose. The purpose proceeds from the faith. What man believes concerning God determines what duty he believes God requires of him.

There were movements toward Church unity in

our Yesterday, but more significant were trends which prepared the way for the ecumenical consciousness which is craving expression in a re-united Christian Church today. The historical study of the Bible revealed differences in detail among New Testament Christians while loyalties and convictions gave them a common faith and a united witness to the world. It also revealed differences in the organization of the Church in various localities without interfering with the Church's united life and service. The social application of the Gospel and the missionary movement brought home the necessity for a united attack upon social sins and a united crusade to make all nations disciples of Christ. The partnership of Christians in philanthropic and reform enterprises and their co-operation in evangelistic campaigns made them aware of their unity in faith and purpose. The study of religious experience disclosed similarities in devotional habit and temperamental kinships between folk of widely sundered ecclesiastical traditions. A closer acquaintance with the worship and educational methods of various communions resulted in much borrowing, so softening differences. Since the Great War, when Christians were shocked at the starkly pagan world in which they found themselves, and under the pressure of anti-religious assaults and persecution, the Church has felt its oneness over against its foes and an urgent desire to compass a visible reunion of its forces for a common front in its warfare and a common witness to its Lord. In a world tumbling to pieces and incapable of furnishing political or economic or intellectual fellowship, the Church has found itself the sole world-wide community, transcending bounds of race and nation and class, and is resolving to be what in God's purpose it is—the inclusive Body of Christ refashioning men after His mind and holding them together in Him.

The necessity under present circumstances of achieving a practical unity among Christians is being recognized by leaders of the Church in almost every land. They would share the mood recently voiced in Westminster Abbey:

The complacency of the rank and file membership in the Churches today is almost incredible, as they sit in the illusion of security in their little denominational dugouts under a long-abandoned no-man's land, while the lines behind them are already broken. Twenty years from now the question will not be whether episcopally ordained clergy are or are not the best kind of ministry. It will be whether there are any Christians or any Churches in which men can minister. A house divided against a house falleth. This is more than a matter of self-preservation. It is that, but that is a sub-Christian motive. It is rather a question of the Church's task and its true vocation in the world, of its loyalty to the purpose of its Founder and the will of God to unite the world in peace.[11]

The need for world fellowship has given the Church a much larger place in the thought of Protestants.[12] The former individualism appears utterly inadequate under present circumstances. The individual cannot hold Christian convictions and live in loyalty to his Lord under a totalitarian State. His own spiritual freedom is bound up with that of the independence of the Church. Men realize that a serious loss occurred at the Reformation when the Churches organized themselves within national frontiers and when in so many lands the State assumed a control in Church affairs. The Church is supranational, and it is intolerable that governments have power to refuse permission to its leaders to meet in ecumenical conference, as happened when Germany declined passports to some of the representatives chosen to Oxford and Edinburgh. Roman Catholicism has wisely maintained its world-wide solidarity and provided for frequent intercourse between its leaders. The Church must be able to marshal all its spiritual forces and witness to the mind of Christ in a situation which affects the peace of mankind.

The question of the relative spheres of Church and State is up for rediscussion, and Christians are reconsidering their duties to Caesar and his dominion and to God and the Divine Society.

New attention is being given to fellowship within the Church. If the Church transcends barriers of race, nation, and class, this must be laid on the consciences of its members and must be manifest in its organization. The Christian of today and tomorrow must be vividly aware of his life in the world-wide communion of followers of Jesus, and place its interests above all others. He must give the Spirit of Christ the chance to rid him of prejudice, intolerance, and every defect of sympathy which renders him narrower in outlook and duller in moral sensitiveness than his Master. While the Church is outwardly still divided, he must have an ecumenical heart and mind.

At Oxford in 1937 the Ecumenical Conference declared:

If war breaks out, then pre-eminently the Church must manifestly be the Church, still united as the one Body of Christ—though the nations wherein it is planted fight each other—consciously offering the same prayers that God's name may be hallowed, His kingdom come, and His will be done in both, or all, of the warring nations. This fellowship of prayer must at all costs remain unbroken.

That resolve is happily being carried out at present.
It is on no large scale, but among leaders who are
using the same petitions based upon the Lord's
Prayer. Both on the eve of the outbreak of hos-
tilities and since intercourse is being maintained.[13]
The almost insuperable difficulties must not be overlooked. The Church has yet far to go to overcome
the all-but-absolute nationalism which prevails in
our present world. Its independent jurisdiction has
to be asserted, and a sphere delimited in which its
authority is recognized by governments.

In periods of conflict the Church has always stif-
fened in steadfastness to the Gospel. When the
world appeared to agree with its ethic and to share
its faith, it was natural that it should freely assimilate current thought and standards. The result was
a mottled Christianity and a Church weakened in
spiritual force. Today it is driven back upon its
divine heritage, is listening with open ears to the
Word of God in Christ, and is sharpening the lines
which separate Christian from pagan. It is never
easy to be both stalwart in fidelity to the distinctive
Christian heritage and hospitable to the message of
the living God through contemporary culture. If
we are reacting from Modernism which was too open
to current influences, we must be careful not to become slaves of tradition. The Church's clew to

God's will is in holding fast to the Christ of yesterday and today.

Our interest is not in adapting the Church to our
time. A recent volume bears the title, *The Church
Against the World.*[14] Conformity, either in opinion
or life, is not Christian. The intransigence of the
Roman Catholic Church gave it a persuasive appeal
to many thoughtful persons in the post-war period.
Vital Protestantism in Germany has declared a
similar *non possumus* over against the demands
of the totalitarian state. Men rightly despise
a chameleon Church taking the color of current
thought and adjusting to the standards of contemporary society. While it must have a *foothold*
in its world, presenting its message to its mind,
rendering its principles relevant to the circumstances
in which men live, laying hold in its worship on
their aspirations and lifting them Godward, it dare
not have *roothold* in it. Its convictions and purposes and powers must derive from above. It has
been written of the early Church:

The resolute renunciation of the world was really the
first thing which made the Church competent and strong
to tell upon the world. Then, if ever, was the saying
true: "He who would do anything for the world must
have nothing to do with it." Revolutions are not ef-
fected with rose water and it was a veritable revolution

to overthrow polytheism and to establish the majesty of God and goodness in the world.[15]

A Church which is at home in society and voices its prevailing views can have nothing redeeming to say to it. It must make its members critics of whatever is in order that they may become creators with Christ of what should be. It has to teach them to do what seems best under existing conditions—the relatively best, in contrast to the absolute judgment of God, and acknowledge its sinfulness. In this awareness of the sin in our human best lies the true way of advance toward the kingdom of God.

In contrast to the Church of Yesterday, the Church of Today seems on the defensive. Then "movements" were the order of the hour—evangelistic campaigns, missionary advances, crusades for social righteousness. Now, with hostile forces threatening her very existence in some lands, and with a new sense of pagan surroundings in lands nominally Christian, she is trying to hold her ground. This is fatal strategy. Age after age the Church has found her life in losing it. A defensive policy is suicidal. She must take the initiative, and move bravely forth to bring the mind of our time—in governments, in commerce and industry, in education and amusements, in the arts and in the family—under the mind of Christ. We need all of Yesterday's hope and enthusiasm, enlightened and deepened by the grim happenings which have intervened, in the Church of Today. If the situation which the present generation of her members faces appears much more alarming, their eyes are opened to the forces of destruction in the world as the eyes of their predecessors were not, and the Church's resources in Christ remain as exhaustless as ever. God is summoning her through the voice of an imperiled day to consecrate all the powers of her whole fellowship to Him for the building of a world in pieces into a new Christendom.

REFERENCES

CHAPTER I

1 — *A Peculiar Treasure*, by EDNA FERBER, p. 2 (Doubleday, Doran & Company, Inc.)

2 — *In Peril of Change*, by C. F. G. MASTERMAN, pp. 167, 168 (Viking Press)

3 — Quoted in G. A. GORDON's *The New Epoch for Faith* (Houghton Mifflin Company)

4 — *The Education of Henry Adams*, p. 330 (Houghton Mifflin Company)

5 — *In Peril of Change*, p. 140 (Viking Press)

6 — *Life of Mrs. Humphry Ward*, by JANET PENROSE TREVELYAN, p. 75 (Dodd, Mead and Company)

7 — *John Fiske, Life and Letters*, by J. S. CLARK, 1:103 note (Houghton Mifflin Company)

8 — *William Graham Sumner*, by HARRIS E. STARR, p. 543 (Henry Holt and Company)

9 — *The Life of Henry Drummond*, by GEORGE ADAM SMITH, p. 224 (Doubleday)

10 — *The Everlasting Reality of Religion*, published in *Christian Literature*, February, 1896, p. 428

11 — *The Idea of God*, by JOHN FISKE, p. 167 (Houghton Mifflin Company)

12 — *The Theology of an Evolutionist*, by LYMAN ABBOTT, p. 178 (Houghton Mifflin Company)

13 — *Constructive Natural Theology*, by NEWMAN SMYTH, p. viii (Scribners)

14 — *The Theology of an Evolutionist*, p. 180 (Houghton Mifflin Company)

15 — *Recollections and Reflections*, by NEWMAN SMYTH, pp 209, 210 (Scribners)

16 — *Through Science to Faith*, LOWELL LECTURES, 1900-1901 (Scribners)

17 — *The Theology of an Evolutionist*, p. 9 (Houghton Mifflin Company)

18 — *Each in His Own Tongue,* by WILLIAM HERBERT CARRUTH (Gorham)

19 — Frederic Myers, quoted in MASTERMAN, *op. cit.,* p. 65 (Viking Press)

20 — *Our Country,* p. 222, *The New Era,* p. 79, by JOSIAH STRONG (Doubleday)

21 — *A Defence of Philosophic Doubt* (Doran and Company)

22 — *Varieties of Religious Experience,* pp. 491, 492 (Longmans)

23 — *The New Epoch for Faith,* p. 49 (Houghton Mifflin and Company)

24 — *The Direct and Fundamental Proofs of the Christian Religion,* p. 149 (Scribners)

25 — *Ibid.,* p. 151

26 — *Ibid.,* p. 171

27 — Cf. JOHN DEWEY, *A Common Faith* (Yale University Press) ; JULIAN HUXLEY, *Religion without Revelation* (Harper and Brothers) —both non-Theists. H. N. WIEMAN in his several books and in *Contemporary American Theology* (Round Table Press) , p. 348, who reaches a Theistic faith

28 — *The Nature of the Physical World,* by A. S. EDDINGTON, p. 338 (Macmillan Company)

29 — *Selected Letters,* by BARON F. VON HUGEL, p. 353 (Dutton)

30 — *Science in Search of God,* by K. MATHER, p. 91 (Henry Holt)

31 — *The Life and Letters of Charles Darwin,* Vol. II, p. 177

32 — *Autobiography,* by H. SPENCER, Vol. II, p. 460 (Appleton)

33 — *Synthetic Philosophy,* quoted by BEATRICE WEBB, *My Apprenticeship,* pp. 87, 88 (Longmans)

34 — *My Apprenticeship,* by BEATRICE WEBB, p. 89 (Longmans)

35 — *The Wonderful Century,* by ALFRED RUSSELL WALLACE, p. 381 (Dodd, Mead and Company)

36 — *Science and the Modern World,* by A. N. WHITEHEAD, pp. 140, 141 (Macmillan Company)

37 — "Evolution and Ethics," *Romanes Lecture,* p. 34 (Appleton)

38 — *Ibid.,* p. 36

39 — Quoted in MASTERMAN, *op. cit.,* 210 (Viking Press)

40 — *Romanes Lecture,* p. 36 (Appleton)

REFERENCES
CHAPTER II

1 — *The Idea of God*, by J. FISKE, p. 116 (Houghton Mifflin Company)

2 — *The Autobiography of Mark Rutherford*, by W. HALE WHITE, p. 18 (Dodd, Mead and Company)

3 — *Recollections*, by WASHINGTON GLADDEN, p. 427 (Houghton Mifflin Company)

4 — *Theology of an Evolutionist*, by LYMAN ABOOTT, p. 184 (Houghton Mifflin Company)

5 — *Ibid.*, p. 10

6 — *The Ascent of Man*, by HENRY DRUMMOND, p. 33 (Pott)

7 — *Endeavours After the Christian Life*, by JAMES MARTINEAU, 2nd Series (Beacon Press)

8 — *The Destiny of Man*, by J. FISKE, p. 103 (Houghton Mifflin Company)

9 — Robert Browning

10 — *The Story of My Life*, by SIR HARRY H. JOHNSTON, p. 460 (Bobbs Merrill Company)

11 — *A Plaint to Man*, by THOMAS HARDY

12 — *The Destiny of Man*, by J. FISKE, pp. 117, 118 (Houghton Mifflin Company)

13 — *The Story of a Varied Life*, by W. S. RAINSFORD, p. 386 (Doubleday)

14 — *The New Theology*, by R. J. CAMPBELL, p. 92 (Macmillan Company)

15 — *The Religion of a Mature Mind*, by GEORGE A. COE, pp. 252, 252 (Revell)

16 — Quoted in C. C. J. WEBB, *Religious Thought in England from 1850*, pp. 55, 56 (Oxford)

17 — *The Programme of Modernism*

18 — *The Rise of Modern Religious Ideas*, by A. C. McGIFFERT, p. 310 (Macmillan Company)

19 — *Varieties of Religious Experience*, by W. JAMES, p. 521 (Longmans)

20 — *The Letters of William James*, Vol. II, p. 214 (Atlantic Monthly Press)

21 — *What Is Christianity?* by A. HARNACK, Eng. tr., pp. 321, 322 (Putnam)

22 — *A Puritan in Babylon*, by WILLIAM ALLEN WHITE, p. 73 (Macmillan Company)

23 — *A Century's Change,* by GEORGE HARRIS, p. 235 (Houghton Mifflin Company)

24 — *Current Christian Thinking,* by GERALD B. SMITH, p. 167 (University of Chicago Press)

25 — *Religious Experience and Scientific Method,* by H. N. WIEMAN, p. 381 (Macmillan Company)

26 — Quoted in C. C. J. WEBB, *Religious Thought in England from 1850,* Oxford, p. 133. J. S. MILL's *Essay on Theism* and H. SPENCER's *Principles of Ethics* (Appleton) strongly affirmed Protestant Christian morality

27 — Cf. *Only Yesterday,* by F. L. ALLEN, p. 94 (Harper and Brothers)

28 — *Sociology,* by JOHN BASCOM (Putnam), p. 264; Cf. his *Social Theory,* Part V (Crowell)

29 — *The World as the Subject of Redemption,* p. 135 (Longmans)

30 — Quoted by MARK SULLIVAN, *Our Times,* Vol. I, p. 364 (Scribners)

31 — *The Idea of the Holy,* RUDOLF OTTO, Eng. tr. (Oxford)

32 — *Selected Letters,* by BARON F. VON HUGEL, p. 353 (Dutton)

33 — *Essay on Intellect,* by R. W. EMERSON

34 — *Heroes of Thought,* by J. MIDDLETON MURRY, p. 5 (Messner)

35 — Isaiah 14: 13-15

CHAPTER III

1 — *My Forty Years in New York,* by CHARLES H. PARKHURST, p. 8 (Macmillan)

2 — *Recollections,* by WASHINGTON GLADDEN, pp. 260, 261 (Houghton Mifflin Company)

3 — *The Heretic's Defence,* by HENRY PRESERVED SMITH, pp. 47, 48 (Scribners)

4 — *Recollections and Reflections,* by NEWMAN SMYTH, Chap. VI (Scribners)

5 — *My Generation,* by WILLIAM J. TUCKER (Houghton Mifflin), Chap. VII; *History of Andover Theological Seminary* by HENRY K. ROWE, Chap. VIII

6 — In the *Observer,* April 16, 1891

7 — In *The Authority of Holy Scriptures,* 3d Ed., pp. 94, 95

REFERENCES

8 — In *Presbyterian Review*, Vol. II, p. 245

9 — In *op. cit.*, p. 95

10 — In the *North American Review*, July, 1891, p. 110

11 — The conservative side is given in *The Briggs Heresy Case*, by JOHN J. McCook, and the Seminary's side in *Another Decade in the History of Union Theological Seminary*, by G. L. PRENTISS

12 — *The Heretic's Defence*, by H. P. SMITH, p. 109 (Scribners)

13 — *Criticism and Dogma*, in *North American Review*, 1906, pp. 861-874

14 — *Randall Davidson*, by G. K. A. BELL, Vol. I, Chap. XLI (Oxford)

15 — *The Case of Professor Gilbert*, in *The Outlook* for Dec. 23, 1899, and May 19, 1900

16 — *For the Benefit of My Creditors*, by HINCKLEY G. MITCHELL, especially pp. 236-253 (Beacon Press)

17 — *Proceedings in the Trial and Appeal of the Rev. Algernon S. Crapsey*, published by Thomas Whittaker, 1906

18 — *A Century's Change*, by GEORGE HARRIS, p. 240 (Houghton Mifflin Company)

19 — *Christianity and Liberalism*, by J. G. MACHEN, pp. 48 ff. (Macmillan Company)

20 — *Dogmatic Theology*, by W. G. T. SHEDD, p. 307 (Scribners)

21 — *The True Humanity of Christ*, by HOWARD CROSBY, p. 23

22 — *The Story of a Varied Life*, by W. S. RAINSFORD, pp. 373, 374 (Doubleday)

23 — *A Century's Change in Religion*, by GEORGE HARRIS, p. 232 (Houghton Mifflin Company)

24 — *Out of My Life and Thought*, by ALBERT SCHWEITZER (Henry Holt), pp. 61, 62; cf. *Die Predigt Jesu vom Reiche Gottes*, by J. WEISS

25 — *The Golden Bough*, 1st ed., 1890 (Macmillan)

26 — *My Generation*, by WILLIAM J. TUCKER, p. 135 (Houghton Mifflin Company)

27 — By ROBERT NORWOOD (Scribners)

28 — *Sixty Years with the Bible*, by W. N. CLARKE, p. 253 (Scribners)

29 — *Ibid.*, pp. 247, 248

30 — *The Validity of the Gospel Record,* by ERNEST FINDLAY SCOTT, pp. 201, 202 (Scribners)

31 — *The Divinity of Jesus Christ,* by JOHN MARTIN CREED, p. 136 (Macmillan Company)

32 — *What Is Christian Education,* by GEORGE A. COE, p. 29 (Scribners)

CHAPTER IV

1 — *The Evidence of Christian Experience,* by LEWIS F. STEARNS, p. 18 (Scribners)

2 — By CHARLES LORING-BRACE, head of the Children's Aid Society

3 — By JAMES S. DENNIS (Revell)

4 — STEARNS, *op. cit.,* p. 18 (Scribners)

5 — *Ibid.,* p. 95

6 — *Ibid.,* p. 195

7 — *Ibid.,* p. 227

8 — *The Psychology of Religion,* by EDWIN D. STARBUCK (Scribners)

9 — *Ibid,* p. ix

10 — *The Varieties of Religious Experience,* by W. JAMES, p. 166 (Longmans)

11 — *Pragmatism,* by W. JAMES, p. 291 f (Longmans)

12 — *A Pluralistic Universe,* by W. JAMES (Longmans), pp. 328, 329. Cf. the Appendix to *Some Problems of Philosophy,* p. 224 (Longmans)

13 — Cf. *The Nature of Religion,* by W. P. PATERSON, pp. 98-110. (Doran)

14 — *The Mind of the Master,* by JOHN WATSON, pp. 131 ff. (Doran)

15 — *The Idea of the Holy,* by R. OTTO, p. 7 (Oxford)

16 — *Ibid.,* p. 10

17 — *Ibid.,* p. 28

18 — *Naturalism and Religion,* by R. OTTO, p. 1 (Putnam)

19 — *Ibid.,* p. 12

20 — By HENRY CHURCHILL KING (Macmillan)

21 — *The Varieties of Religious Experiences,* by W. JAMES (Longmans), p. 58, quoted by OTTO in *The Idea of the Holy* (Oxford)

REFERENCES

22 — *Letters,* by W. JAMES, Vol. II (Atlantic Monthly Press)
23 — *Ibid.,* Vol. II, p. 127
24 — Quoted as by Clark Maxwell in H. C. King, *op. cit.,* p. 47 (Macmillan)
25 — *The Mystery of Religion,* by EVERETT DEAN MARTIN, p. 26 (Harper and Brothers)
26 — *Theories of Religious Experience,* p. 187 (Round Table Press)
27 — *The Interpretation of Religion,* p. 232 (Scribners)
28 — *De Praedestinatione Sanctorum,* Sec. 5.
29 — *Communion with God,* Eng. tr., pp. 283, 284 (Putnam)
30 — *The Two Sources of Morality and Religion* (Henry Holt)
31 — *The Letters of George Tyrrell,* p. 113
32 — *God in These Times,* by H. P. VAN DUSEN, p. 71 (Scribners)
33 — Isaiah 64:7
34 — *Is a Christian Philosophy a Contradiction in Terms?* by DAVID E. ROBERTS in *The Journal of Religion,* April, 1939

CHAPTER V

1— *My Forty Years in New York,* by CHARLES H. PARKHURST, pp. 109 ff. (Macmillan and Company)
2 — *William James and Other Essays,* by JOSIAH ROYCE, p. 30 (Macmillan and Company)
3 — *Recollections,* by WASHINGTON GLADDEN, p. 63 (Houghton Mifflin Company)
4 — In *Bibliotheca Sacra,* July, 1892
5 — WASHINGTON GLADDEN, *op. cit.* (Houghton Mifflin Company)
6 — *My Generation,* by WILLIAM J. TUCKER, pp. 178-180 (Houghton and Company)
7 — "Notes of the Progress of the Social Conscience," in the *Atlantic Monthly*
8 — *The Gospel for an Age of Doubt,* by HENRY VAN DYKE, pp. 299, 300 (Macmillan Company)
9 — *Our Times,* by MARK SULLIVAN, Vol. II, p. 316 (Scribners)
10 — *Ibid.,* pp. 292, 293
11 — By H. D. LLOYD, 1892 (Harper and Brothers)
12 — *The Christian State,* by GEORGE D. HERRON, pp. 15-17
13 — *Ibid.,* p. 31

14 — *Our Times,* by MARK SULLIVAN, Vol. I, p. 131 (Scribners)

15 — *Ibid.* pp., 195, 196

16 — *Ibid.,* pp. 183, 184

17 — *Christianity and the Social Crisis,* by W. RAUSCHENBUSCH, p. xiii (Macmillan Company)

18 — *Ibid.,* pp. 149, 150

19 — *Christianizing the Social Order,* p. 464 (Macmillan Company)

20 — "The Church and the Social Crisis," in the *Presbyterian Tribune,* July 6, 1939, p. 7

21 — "The New Reservation of Time," by WILLIAM J. TUCKER, in the *Atlantic Monthly,* September, 1915

22 — *Sin and Society,* by EDWARD A. ROSS, Chap. V (Houghton Mifflin Company)

23 — Hymn by FRANCIS H. ROWLEY, written in 1886, included in *Gospel Hymns,* by IRA D. SANKEY, 1887

24 — *Ultimate Conceptions,* by GEORGE A. GORDON, p. 372 (Houghton Mifflin Company)

25 — *Rise of Modern Religious Ideas,* by A. C. MCGIFFERT, p. 276 (Macmillan Company)

26 — *The Psychology of Religion,* by GEORGE A. COE, p. 243 (University of Chicago Press)

27 — By NORMAN ANGELL

28 — *Randall Davidson,* by G. K. A. BELL, Vol. I, pp. 655, 656 (Oxford)

29 — So much misinformation has been spread concerning the American Churches in the Great War that we are fortunate in possessing the record from the accurate pen of W. A. BROWN in *A Teacher and His Times,* pp. 223-250 (Scribners)

30 — *The Letters of T. E. Lawrence,* p. 262

31 — *In Place of Profit,* by HARRY F. WARD (Scribners)

32 — *The Good Society,* by WALTER LIPPMANN, p. 382 (Little, Brown)

CHAPTER VI

1 — *Adolescence,* by G. STANLEY HALL (Appleton)

2 — *My Generation,* by W. J. TUCKER, p. 168 (Houghton Mifflin Company)

3 — Cf. LOUIS F. BENSON, *The Hymnody of the Christian Church* (Doran) (1928), ARCHIBALD T. DAVISON, *Prot-*

REFERENCES

estant Church Music in America (1933) (Scribners),
CHARLES WINFRED DOUGLAS, *Church Music in History and
Practice* (1937) (Scribners)

4 — Cf. GEORGE A. COE, *The Spiritual Life* (1900) (Methodist
Book Concern

5 — *The Age of Confidence,* by HENRY S. CANBY, p. 133 (Farrar)

6 — *Contemporary American Philosophers,* by RALPH BARTON
PERRY, Vol. 2, p. 208

7 — *Aspects of the Infinite Mystery,* by GEORGE A. GORDON, p.
94 (Houghton Mifflin Company)

8 — *The Rise of Modern Religious Ideas,* by A. C. McGIFFERT,
p. 303 (The Macmillan Company)

9 — *The Religion of a Mature Mind,* by GEORGE A. COE, pp.
106, 107 (Revell)

10 — *Jesus, Lord or Leader,* by FRANK LENWOOD, 1930 (Harper
and Brothers)

11 — *Convictions,* by F. R. BARRY, pp. 93, 94 (Nisbet)

12 — No more significant autobiography on the subject can be
read than that of my colleague, WILLIAM ADAMS BROWN,
A Teacher and His Times (Scribners)

13 — *Federal Council Bulletin,* November 1939, pp. 3, 4.

14 — *The Church Against the World,* by NIEBUHR, PAUCK, and
MILLER (Willett)

15 — *The Mission and Expansion of Christianity,* by A. HAR-
NACK, Eng. tr., Vol. I, p. 98 (Putnam)